A Charismatic
Truce

A Charismatic Truce

DAVID SHIBLEY

Thomas Nelson Inc., Publishers
Nashville   New York

Library of Congress Cataloging in Publication Data

Shibley, David.
  A charismatic truce.

  Includes bibliographical references.
  1. Pentecostalism. I. Title.
BR1644.S53   270.8'2   78-10469
ISBN 0-8407-5663-1

Dedicated to the Trinity Temple
Bible Church in Fort Smith, who
by the grace of God joyfully worship together in the warm climate
of a charismatic truce.

Contents

Acknowledgements

I owe a debt of gratitude to so many: to my wonderful wife Naomi for her prayers, patience, and insights; to Debbie Sandusky who labored diligently on the manuscript; to Dr. William Bennett, Rev. Jim Burkett, Dr. Charles Farah, and Dr. Jerry Horner for some very enlightening interviews; to Peter Gillquist whose writings helped mold my thinking into a central stance on the charismatic issue; and to my dear parents who modeled for me a balanced Pentecostalism.

Introduction

For years now the phenomenon commonly referred to as the charismatic movement has been one of the hottest issues in Christendom. Unfortunately, it is also one of the most divisive topics today among Christians. Just mention the term "charismatic" and you will get some kind of response. To many it is a red-flag word. To many others it is the label for those of like precious experience.

Some have written off these modern charismatic occurrences as completely of the devil. Others have declared the movement to be the greatest renewal in the church since the Reformation. Obviously there is a wide diversity of opinion! Both the Scriptures and history convince me that either a blanket endorsement or a blanket rejection of the charismatic movement is a simplistic cop-out. It is to bury one's head in the sand doctrinally. However, the issue is too complex to draw conclusions from casual observance—either outside or inside the movement.

Perhaps only a few will be in total agreement with all the points I make in this book. Some will claim I have afforded the charismatic position too much. Others will say, too little. Still others will accuse me of compromise. However, it has been my purpose to set forth what I believe to be a balanced view of the charismatic phenomenon. I have tenaciously tried to guard against any presuppositions that would tip the scale of my teaching on the Holy Spirit's person and work.

The Bible itself is certainly not a book of compromise. It is, however, a book of balance. Often the issues that divide Christians are a result of tipping the delicately balanced scales of what the Bible is really saying. Just as the proverbial butcher added his thumb to the weight of the meat on the scale, we sometimes pressure Bible verses on the person and work of the Holy Spirit out of context and proportion. We tip the scales. Too often we give more weight and authority to some aspects of the Spirit's work than what the Bible gives. At other times we do not give some workings of the Spirit their proper emphasis. God is not pleased with these practices. "A false balance is abomination to the Lord: But a just weight is His delight" (Prov. 11:1). If we would merely be scriptural we would see that the scales of Bible teaching on the Holy Spirit and His gifts are perfectly balanced.

When one pleads for balance he will be criticized, of course, by those whose off-balance base affects their spiritual equilibrium. No doubt we are all guilty of this at times. In the Civil War there was a soldier who was in partial sympathy with both the Union and the Confederacy. He declared his convictions by wearing a gray coat and blue pants. The result: He was shot at from both sides! I ask my fellow Christians on both sides not to shoot at my "strange uniform" but to read with discernment and grace. What I am offering is a charismatic truce—a central approach that I pray will bring healing to the self-inflicted wounds in Christ's body, the church.

David Shibley

Fort Worth, Texas
1978

1

In the Same Ball Park

The charismatic movement has blessed, encouraged, thrilled, confused, angered, and disillusioned millions of people. In the last decade it has been the cause of more church renewal and more church splits than any other current force in Christendom. It is front-page news among Christians everywhere.

The Pentecostal experience of speaking in tongues began to leap across denominational boundaries with noticeable frequency in the early sixties. A staid Episcopal congregation led by Dennis Bennett was one of the first to experience the phenomenon of *glossolalia* (speaking in tongues) on a large scale outside the boundaries of Pentecostal denominations. Fanned by the ministries of Oral Roberts, David DuPlessis, the Full Gospel Business Men's Fellowship, David Wilkerson, and others, what came to be known as the charismatic movement spread rapidly. In fact many have thought it spread like "wildfire."

By the end of the decade the impossible was happening; people of every doctrinal stripe and background were worshiping together under a common banner of having received the baptism in the Holy Spirit. Some church leaders proclaimed a new day of fellowship and power, while others looked on with suspicion and even alarm. To complicate the issue for some (and to brighten it for others), the charismatic flame not only leaped through Protestant ranks but into Roman Catholicism as well. It was, to say the least, unprecedented.

Statistics vary on how widespread the charismatic movement really is. Almost everyone agrees, however, that there are several million charismatics in America. Some estimates go up to ten million. Possibly up to two-and-one-half million of these are Roman Catholic. It would be intriguing to read a future church historian's observation regarding the charismatic movement of the 1970s and 1980s. Something of great importance has happened in the last twenty-five years, and its full impact and importance will not be known in our lifetime.

If you are like me, you grow weary of terms. Yet it is vitally important to deal with terminology as it relates to the charismatic issue. In fact, an unwillingness to struggle with the semantics problems between charismatics and noncharismatics has contributed to misunderstanding and distrust between the two groups.

For instance, evangelicals and charismatics are often talking past each other when they speak of the "baptism" in the Holy Spirit. To many mainline evangelicals this term refers to an act of the Spirit *at* conversion.* To the charismatic it is the label to describe an enduement of power that is experienced

---

*This is not necessarily true of evangelicals in the American holiness movement, as we shall see later.

after conversion. This is illustrative of the many word difficulties that must be overcome before dialogue can occur effectively between these groups. If we are to experience a charismatic truce, we must come to terms with terms!

So, who or what is a charismatic? Or a Pentecostal? Or an evangelical? What is the baptism in the Holy Spirit? The following explanations should help answer these questions.

Charismatic

The word *charismatic* comes from the Greek word *charisma,* which simply means a freely given and unmerited gift or favor. It is interesting to note that the sister Greek word *charis* means grace. We are dealing with spiritual graces, that is, spiritual gifts. They are sovereign bestowals to believers as an expression of the grace of God. Just as God's greatest gift, salvation, is by grace, so the spiritual gifts are by grace. In the early centuries of the church, when an adult was baptized, the bishop or elder in charge would lay hands on the new convert as he or she came up out of the water. Prayer was offered that this new Christian would receive the baptism or fulness in the Holy Spirit. To use the ancients' term, the believer was *charismated.*

As used today the term "charismatic" most often refers to one who emphasizes the importance of the gifts of the Holy Spirit (particularly tongues and healing) for all Christians. Such a person claims a baptism in the Spirit, which is more often than not accompanied by speaking in tongues. Sometimes charismatics are also labeled as "Neo-

Pentecostals." Thus the charismatic movement is a force within Christendom made up of "charismatics."

It must be pointed out, however, that the Bible teaches that every Christian is truly charismatic. Every Christian has at least one gift sovereignly bestowed by the Holy Spirit as a personal spiritual birthright. First Corinthians 12:7 reads, "But the manifestation of the Spirit is given to *every* man to profit withal" (emphasis mine). But today the term "charismatic" usually refers to one who aligns with the charismatic movement, and that is the way the term will be used in this book.

Other Christians often scorn the charismatics for being "experience-oriented." But this really isn't true of most people who speak in tongues. They are evangelicals first of all, so they seek the truth rather than some emotional thrill. They study the Scriptures to discern God's will for their lives, and they rely on Scriptures to test the validity of their experience.

For example, consider the testimony of John L. Sherrill. As an editor for *Guideposts* magazine, he was doing some research on the charismatic movement in the autumn of 1960. The more he studied the Bible and talked with charismatics, the more he became convinced that the gift of tongues was genuine. He desired it for himself. And as charismatic friends gathered in an Atlantic City hotel room to pray with him, he received the gift. Four years later he wrote:

> . . . One principal change has taken place in my attitude toward the Baptism in the Holy Spirit and

toward speaking in tongues. With each year I have become less emotional about them; with each year I have become more convinced of their value.[1]

By far the majority of charismatics would agree with Sherrill. They have an objective attitude toward the gift of tongues. They are level-headed people. They are reasonable. They study the Bible and endeavor to live by it. But because charismatics have experienced a supernatural gift that other evangelicals don't understand, charismatics are thought to be strange.

Granted, some charismatics exercise their gift in an emotional frenzy. They seek tongues as an emotional "high." But these people are on the fringe of the charismatic movement, and we shouldn't judge all charismatics by them.

It's difficult to get a clear picture of the charismatic movement because many charismatics keep their gift to themselves. Untold numbers of Christians speak in tongues only at home because they believe it is a private prayer language. So think twice before you call charismatics "weird" or "fanatical." You may be talking about your boss, a friend, or even your pastor! You might have a better appreciation of the charismatic movement if you realized how many charismatics you know.

Charismatics have contributed a great deal to the life of the church. For one thing, they have reminded all Christians that the Holy Spirit *does* grant spiritual gifts. Certainly not all Christians speak in tongues or have the gift of miracles or healing. Paul suggested as much in 1 Corinthians 12:29,30. But this is just the beauty of it. Christ's body is every bit as diverse in its membership as is your body or mine. Speaking of the church, Paul says in Ephesians 4:16 that ". . . from whom [Christ] the whole body fitly joined together and compacted by that which every joint supplieth, according to the effectual working in every part, maketh increase of the body unto the edifying of itself in love."

Still, a lot of Christians would never call themselves charismatics because they do not wish to be identified with the charismatic movement. They believe the movement gives too much emphasis to gifts, an area which they feel the Bible emphasizes very little. But the truth is, the term 'charismatic" is a perfectly scriptural word, one which *every* Christian can wear with gratitude to the Lord. God has gifted children!

Some noncharismatics (as the term is generally used) believe certain gifts of the Holy Spirit claimed by charismatics have, in fact, ceased—or at least no longer function in their New Testament sense. These folks think modern-day occurrences of tongues or miracles are fabricated and are in no way linked to the biblical display of these gifts.

On the other hand, there are many others who are more than happy to be labeled with the charismatic movement. They believe the gifts of the Spirit have been underemphasized to the church's detriment, and now God has sovereignly brought them to the forefront again.

So there you have it. Charismatic. Most of us have used the word at one time or another. The trick is to use it correctly.

Evangelical

Much is heard today about an evangelical renaissance. Truly, the evangelical wing of Christendom is booming in a lot of ways. Evangelical churches are growing while many liberal churches are dying. Evangelical books are selling rapidly. In 1976, Americans elected an evangelical president. Conversions of well-known people make front-page news. At present it is almost stylish for movie stars, ex-gangsters, athletes, and politicians to refer to being "born again."

Isn't it fascinating to read almost weekly in a newspaper or magazine an honest, new attempt by journalists to describe to the public what it means to be "born again"? Everyone seems to be talking about this experience. And I'm glad they are, because it is a very important foundation of New Testament faith. Jesus said to Nicodemus in John 3:3, "Verily, verily I say unto thee, Except a man be born again he cannot see the kingdom of God." To be born again is to repent of sin and trust Jesus Christ as personal Savior. This is the common meeting ground of all evangelicals—charismatics and noncharismatics alike.

Evangelicals, in the modern sense, are people who have experienced a new birth in Christ. Obviously this includes both those who are charismatic and those who aren't. Their theology is primarily traditional and orthodox. Evangelicals agree that the Bible is the final authority in matters of faith and practice. Evangelicals believe that Jesus was born of a virgin, lived a sinless life, died an atoning death,

21

was physically resurrected, ascended to the right hand of the Father, and will one day return in power and glory.

Three sister words to evangelical are *evangel, evangelism,* and *evangelistic. Evangel* simply means the "message," with special reference to the gospel of Christ. *Evangelism* is the proclamation of the gospel with direct reference to transmitting it to unbelievers. To be *evangelistic* is to be about the task of sharing the gospel of Jesus Christ with the unconverted.

There are several shades of evangelicalism. In fact, there is currently debate over who can actually be called an evangelical. Some evangelicals believe in the eternal security of believers, and some don't. Many are premillennial, but some aren't. Some speak in tongues; others don't. Yes, evangelicalism is a diverse community. In this diversity lies both its greatest strength and its greatest weakness.

Evangelicalism is strong when it presents a united front, as in the case of many churches working together to sponsor a Billy Graham Crusade. It is weak, however, when doctrinal distinctives become too broad to represent a unique force in Christendom.

The best example of this combined strength and weakness is the Statement of Faith of the National Association of Evangelicals. The statement is narrow enough so that all who sign it in good conscience must espouse a conservative, evangelical theology. Yet it is broad enough that Baptists who are noncharismatics and Pentecostals who certainly emphasize the charismatic dimension—Brethren who are Calvinists and Nazarenes who are Arminians—can all sign it. The very fact that both charismatics and noncharismatics are evangelicals points to this beauty of inclusiveness that also may suggest an inherent weakness.

The weakness is that evangelicals often tangle their theological roots in the quest for unity, and disrupt the logic of their theology.

Yet at two points of doctrine all evangelicals *should* and do agree: (1) All evangelicals believe that the Bible is our source and standard of truth, and (2) all evangelicals believe that a person must repent of sin and accept Jesus Christ as Savior and Lord.

Evangelicals include Baptists, Nazarenes, Pentecostals, most of the independent churches, and many others—basically the conservative wing of Protestantism. But there are also evangelicals in the liberal churches. In addition, there are many evangelical Catholics (though some evangelicals would think this a contradiction in terms). These renewed, reborn Catholics are sometimes referred to (by themselves and others) as "Billy Graham Catholics." While they often remain faithful to the Roman Catholic Church, they have experienced a new birth in Christ by grace through faith. These born-again Catholics are prime prospects for becoming charismatic Catholics. In fact, it is often true that these evangelical Catholics are won to saving faith in Christ by charismatic Catholics. It is then natural for the new initiate to follow his friend in receiving an experience of speaking in tongues, or *glossolalia.*

Now—think with me—almost all charismatics are doctrinally evangelical. But the inverse is not

23

true by a long shot. Not all evangelicals are charismatic; in fact, a majority are not. Here is where the battle rages: between noncharismatic evangelicals and charismatics (most of whom are also evangelical). It is an intra-evangelical dispute. It is a family feud.

For some reason liberal churches have not opposed the charismatics as actively as the evangelicals have. The liberals' response has usually been either passive, mildly skeptical, or mildly supportive. Although the charismatics have infiltrated their ranks, sometimes with immense repercussions, there has never been much severe opposition from the liberal churches. This is probably best explained by the fact that liberals, by definition, are inclusive theologically. Their response seems to be, "If he wants to speak in tongues, who am I to stop him?" Yet the mental rift between the charismatic in a liberal church and the hierarchy of his church is usually extremely wide. While the liberal would probably deny miracles, the charismatic says he has experienced a miracle—or many miracles. It would seem this might present grave problems, but generally the liberal churches have adapted well to the charismatic phenomenon.

Evangelicals, on the other hand, have not rolled with the charismatic punches so easily. Since there is more of a concern for soundness of doctrine among evangelicals than among liberals, the charismatic movement has been carefully scrutinized by the evangelical camp. Many have concluded that while the charismatic experience may be exhilarating, its muscles lack biblical tone. The charismatics counter that the Bible has become a fresh and living book to them because of their experience with the Holy Spirit. The battle rages on. To the detriment of world evangelization and a united evangelical front, the charismatics and the noncharismatics continue to battle at the flanks.

This is certainly indicative that *neither group's reaction to the other has been Spirit-filled.* I would say it is a tie ballgame as to which group has been nastier. I've heard spokesmen from both groups claim the other group is victimized by demonic influence. One side claims the *full* gospel; the other claims the *true* gospel. The result is that the devil laughs and the world is confused.

Though charismatic evangelicals and non-charismatic evangelicals disagree on many points, they agree on at least two points: (1) The final authority on any doctrinal issue is the Bible, and (2) a person becomes a Christian by repenting and placing personal faith in Jesus Christ as Savior. They may be opposed on many issues, but they are in the same ball park. When confronted with a theological question a charismatic and noncharismatic evangelical will both head for the nearest Bible. They may come up with different answers, but at least they start with the same assumption about where truth is found.

It is relatively easy for me to discontinue fellowship with a liberal over a doctrinal disagreement, because we do not have the same *authority* base. Mine is the Bible; his is subjective reason. However, traditional evangelicals and charismatics both have the same authority base: the Bible. Therefore, most of our doctrinal disagreements are not a question of authority but of *interpretation.* I find it much harder

25

to break fellowship over doctrinal disagreements *if* the authority base is the same. The other person's interpretation may be right. Mine may be right. But we agree on where to play the game. The ball park is within the confines of the Bible. Anything other than the Bible is out of bounds.

Pentecostal

Let's review the historical background of modern Pentecostalism.[2] Really we must go back to the eighteenth century and the teachings of John Wesley. This great English reformer believed there was a "second work of grace" after conversion. He believed that in this "second work" the Christian receives the Holy Spirit, who cleanses the heart from all sin. Wesley believed this experience always came after conversion. He felt that sanctification was an experience for every believer to seek, because it perfected a Christian's relationship with God.

This doctrine was popularized by Charles Finney, the great American revival preacher of the mid-1800s. It became the rallying cry of the post-Civil War revivals, which produced the Church of the Nazarene, the Christian and Missionary Alliance, the Church of God (Anderson, Indiana), and many other noncharismatic holiness churches, which collectively are called the American holiness movement.

Around the turn of the century, a number of Christians began to experience *glossolalia* (speaking in tongues) in connection with this "second work of grace." At first, most of these people were connected with the American holiness movement, but very soon they emerged as a separate group. They called themselves "Pentecostals" because they believed the Holy Spirit had given them the gift of tongues as a sign, as He had done with the apostles on the Day of Pentecost. The Pentecostal movement took root during a series of revival meetings at a Methodist church on Azusa Street in Los Angeles in April 1906. The movement has grown rapidly, and today there are several strong Pentecostal denominations such as the Assemblies of God, the Pentecostal Holiness Church, and the Church of God (Cleveland, Tennessee).

Please note the difference between a Pentecostal church and a holiness church, because many people think these terms are synonymous. It's true that Pentecostals have the same theological heritage as the American holiness movement. But it's a mistake to say that every holiness church is Pentecostal. And it's just as wrong to assume that every Pentecostal church teaches Wesleyan holiness doctrine. Donald W. Dayton says,

> I would suggest that the term "holiness" be used to describe conservative, revivalistic Wesleyanism and "pentecostal" be used to describe those groups that see the baptism of the Holy Spirit accompanied by the experience of "speaking in tongues." This would make perfect sense out of the name Pentecostal Holiness Church, the group with which Oral Roberts was formerly associated. This group does merge a holiness view of sanctification with a pentecostal view of glossolalia, but not all Pentecostal groups are Wesleyan or holiness in understanding. The Assemblies of God, for example, are more "baptistic."[3]

Still another group appeared just after World War II. It was made up of people who had received the gift of tongues *outside* the Pentecostal denominations. Some were members of noncharismatic evangelical churches. Some were members of mainline liberal denominations. Some were Catholics. Some were members of no church body at all. But they felt a close tie to one another because of their common experience of speaking in tongues. They were called "Neo-Pentecostals," and although they had no formal organization they began meeting one another through groups like the Full Gospel Business Men's Fellowship International.

In recent years the Neo-Pentecostal movement has become known as the charismatic movement. There are several charismatic schools, radio and TV stations, and publications. But they are independent of one another, so the group as a whole should still be called a "movement" rather than a denomination or a confederation.

What binds the classical Pentecostal and the new charismatic together is a common experience of speaking in tongues. The experience may be the same, but the subcultural mores of the two groups are often strikingly different. This is vividly seen at almost any charismatic gathering, especially in the appearance of the women.

In one chair is a chic charismatic Presbyterian with the latest look in makeup, wearing an attractive pantsuit. Seated next to her is a college-age girl who looks like a holdover from the Jesus movement. Her blue jeans are faded and her sandals are old. Across her not-so-concealing tee shirt is printed "Praise The Lord!" On the other side of her is a woman who has never known what it is to wear a pantsuit or jeans. Her dress has always come down past her knees and still does. Whether it's fashionable or not is unimportant. She wears no makeup. Her hair is raised heavenward in the "Pentecostal Bun" hairstyle made famous by Vestel Goodman. She contrasts sharply with the other two women. But to her, this outward conservatism is important. It means she is not conformed to the world; she is concerned about holiness. As she glances at the other two she is bewildered. She ponders how they can have a "holiness" experience with evidently little or no concern for what she, at least, considers to be holiness. If evangelicals overall are a wide and diversified group, it would seem the charismatics are even more so.

Although there is a definite bond between classic Pentecostals and charismatics, there are distinct differences. The classic Pentecostal generally gives more weight to the necessity of speaking in tongues by an insistence (not just a suggestion) that tongues are *the* evidence of being filled or baptized in the Spirit. The classic Pentecostal also has severe difficulty accepting the validity of an experience of speaking in tongues among some charismatics who have not met certain standards of holiness that the Pentecostal deems highly important.

So it is easy to imagine the shock wave that swept through traditional Pentecostalism in 1968 when Oral Roberts removed himself from the Pentecostal Holiness Church and joined the United Methodists. At the time I was living in Tulsa and was a high school classmate of his youngest daughter, Roberta.

I was taking three or four kids home one evening

29

from a Youth For Christ rally. Roberta was one of them. Suddenly, in the middle of the conversation, she said, "David, tomorrow my parents are joining Boston Avenue Methodist Church."

I'm glad she was in the back seat so she couldn't see my expression. My mouth dropped open in amazement and disbelief. My heart was utterly grieved. Because of my conservative Pentecostal background, a thousand thoughts flashed through my mind: He's gone liberal; we've lost our leader; it's an ecumenical plot!

Today, a decade later, I simply believe the reason he has given for changing: The Lord told him to do it. I believe time has vindicated him and shown the wisdom of his move. But many old-line Pentecostals remain unconvinced. Some of them still view him and all the charismatics from mainline denominations with skepticism. And because of my Pentecostal upbringing, I sympathize with them. It's not an easy thing to watch the Holy Spirit work in churches and groups you have always viewed as compromising and unbiblical.

Although they may sometimes feel they have given birth to an uncomely child, the Pentecostal churches are the "mother" of the modern charismatic movement. From them, an experience and mode of worship began to infiltrate many of the more traditional churches. Baptists, Lutherans, Methodists, and others began to share a common experience with Pentecostals, though many of these new charismatics have remained in their original denominations. In fact, this is the philosophy espoused in the Full Gospel Business Men's Fellowship International: Stay in your denomination and help others come into the fullness of the Spirit.

So not all charismatics are Pentecostals. There are Methodist charismatics, Episcopalian charismatics, charismatics of other denominations, and, if you will pardon the redundancy, Pentecostal charismatics. The new charismatics, the classical Pentecostals—these together make up the broadly based charismatic movement.

Baptism in the Holy Spirit

John the Baptist used the phrase "baptize in the Holy Spirit" to describe the ministry of Christ (see Mark 1:8, Matt. 3:11, and Luke 3:16). John was pointing the people away from himself to Jesus, the Lamb of God, who would take away the sins of the world and baptize them in the Holy Spirit. As to when or how this baptism would happen, these passages are silent.

Many evangelicals believe the baptism in the Holy Spirit occurs when one is saved. In other words, they believe the act of the Spirit's baptizing us into Christ is part of regeneration. However, this does not exclude the belief among evangelicals that there can be an experience *after* salvation during which the Holy Spirit takes complete control of the life of a Christian for the first time. This is a key doctrine of the holiness churches. Variously they refer to it as the baptism in the Spirit and as the *filling* of the Spirit. In fact, most evangelicals would concede to the possibility of a post-conversion filling of the Spirit. The problem is, to a large degree, a semantic difference in the usage of terms among charismatics and noncharismatics. And frankly, there seems to be scriptural warrant for the use of either term, baptism or filling, to refer to the experience of an enduement of heavenly power.

Luke records the experience of the one hundred and twenty on the Day of Pentecost in these words: "And they were all *filled* with the Holy Ghost . . ." (Acts 2:4, emphasis mine). Jesus, speaking of the same forthcoming incident said, ". . . you shall be *baptized* with the Holy Ghost . . ." (Acts 1:5, emphasis mine). It seems clear that both words, baptism and filling, are used to describe the same event.

There is a real difference of opinion, however, on what evidence will accompany this experience. Most charismatics believe the experience is usually accompanied by speaking in tongues or that tongues will be experienced shortly thereafter. I think I would be safe in saying that seventy-five percent or more of all charismatics believe that though one does not *have* to speak in tongues to receive the "baptism" in the Holy Spirit, it certainly would be considered the norm.

This term—"baptism in the Holy Spirit"—has been used in America for over one hundred years. Most early leaders of the American holiness movement said that a person received the Holy Spirit in a "second blessing" or a "second crisis" after conversion. Others preferred to call it "a second work of grace," as John Wesley had done. A Congregationalist holiness writer, Asa Mahan, was probably the first to call the experience "baptism in the Holy Spirit."

The holiness writers didn't necessarily use different terms to imply a difference of doctrine, although we can detect some subtle shades of meaning in the terms they used. But an interesting change in terms has taken place. I will use Moody Bible Institute as an illustration, but you'll find this trend is common among traditional evangelicals.

Close to the turn of the century, two of the great spokesmen for Christianity in America were Dwight L. Moody and R. A. Torrey, who served respectively as the first and second presidents of Moody Bible Institute in Chicago. Moody and Torrey also referred to an enduement with supernatural power *subsequent* to salvation. They spoke of this experience as the "baptism" of the Holy Spirit because they believed it was vital to a victorious Christian life. The school they founded is one of the most highly respected of all evangelical institutions. Yet M.B.I. is certainly not a charismatic school. The teachers there now would refer to what Moody called "the baptism" as the "filling" of the Holy Spirit. Does the change in terms indicate a change in theology? Perhaps. But to a greater extent I think it indicates that traditional evangelicals don't want to be identified with charismatics, who commonly speak of the "baptism in the Holy Spirit." I think the folks at Moody have stopped talking about the "baptism" in the Holy Spirit because they don't want to sound like charismatics. Many traditional evangelicals have done that.

However, we should not conclude that the major difficulty is just in the definition of terms. Though terms are a good deal of the problem, they are not the whole problem. Things go deeper than that.

33

There is a distinct *doctrinal* difference between charismatics and noncharismatics regarding the nature of the gifts of the Holy Spirit. So let us now turn to see exactly what it is that charismatic Christians believe and teach.

------

[1]John L. Sherrill, *They Speak with Other Tongues* (New York: Pyramid Books, 1965), p. 127.

[2]Frederick Dale Bruner gives an excellent account of this history in *A Theology of the Holy Spirit* (Grand Rapids, Mich.: William B. Eerdmans, 1970), pp. 35-55.

[3]Donald W. Dayton, *The American Holiness Movement: A Bibliographic Introduction* (Wilmore, Kentucky: B. L. Fisher Library, 1970), p. 25.

2

What the Charismatics Are Saying

In his journal entry for November 25, 1759, John
Wesley noted special outpourings of the Holy Spirit
and expressed the opinion that the danger was less
in overemphasis than in suppression of spiritual
phenomena. His insight is certainly needed today:

> The danger was to regard extraordinary circum-
> stances too much, such as outcries, convulsions, vi-
> sions, trances, as if these were essential to the in-
> ward work. . . . Perhaps the danger is, to regard
> them too little; to condemn them altogether; to imag-
> ine they had nothing of God in them, and were a
> hinderance to his work. . . . At first it was, doubtless,
> wholly from God. It is partly so at this day; and He
> will enable us to discern how far, in every case, the
> work is pure and where it mixes or degenerates.[1]

To miss the Holy Spirit is certainly more to be
feared than to misunderstand the Holy Spirit. But
the sheer strength of numbers is forcing the whole
church to sit up and listen to what the charismatics
are saying. What the church will hear from them
are mighty praises to the Lord, a for-real belief in a
God who performs the impossible, and a refreshing
abandon-mentality that seems to say, "If the Bible

teaches it, do it—with no questions asked." They are reminiscent of Moody and his total abandon to the will of God.

One morning, as Moody and Torrey were having breakfast in the seventh story of a Chicago hotel, Moody remarked, "Torrey, if I thought God wanted me to jump out of that window, I'd jump!" In this respect charismatics seem more akin to Moody than to contemporary traditional evangelicals.

Every Christian should thank God for the charismatic element within the church. In times like these we need a God who performs the incredible. The charismatics are reminding us we still have One who does.

Of the many voices in the church today, the charismatics seem to be the most vocal and convincing. From my observation they are leading the way in the areas of Christian radio and television and in Christian music. They are becoming a major contributor to the Christian book market with several new charismatic publishing houses.

It is no secret, by the way, that a lot of ink is being wasted on not-so-hot evangelical books that are coming off the presses in droves. In my opinion the charismatic sector of evangelical books does its share of producing this waste of paper and ink. Some books by charismatic authors are quite beneficial, but many books seem to follow a thin, "True Confessions" format: "I was a teen-age, defeated Christian. Then I received the gift of speaking in tongues. My new prayer language now enables me to live in victory. This can happen to you too!"

Myriads of Christians are buying their message. Like the devotees to John the Baptist, the uninformed believer's response to such testimonies is often, "We have not so much as heard whether there be any Holy Ghost" (Acts 19:2). They may say, "Our pastor didn't tell us. Our church never discusses it. This is something new—and exciting!" And by the thousands each year there are new inductees into the charismatic movement.

The main message of the charismatics to the church is this: Put the Holy Spirit back into the Trinity! The church is more often than not fruitless and powerless. Sadly, many churches seem to want to stay that way. They know there is a safety risk tied to the use of power, and they are not willing to take the risk. And although it is bad when an outsider comes in and says we are crazy, it is worse when a visitor comes in and says we are dead!

The securely established church has fearfully overreacted to the charismatics' zeal. There is no doubt in my mind that the outbreak of charismatic gifts was ordained by God to bring renewal to a weakened church. But by and large the church powers-that-be have not interpreted it that way. Like all humans, churchmen have a fear of the unknown. The only difference is that traditional churchmen seem to have this fear in astounding proportions.

The church of the Lord was born and nurtured in a spiritually revolutionary climate. It was the belief of the early Christians (a belief that the Bible affirms) that they were to counter the status quo, not be a part of it. John said, "Love not the world . . ." (1 John 2:15). Paul said, "Be not conformed to this world . . ." (Rom. 12:2). James warned that "friendship of the world is enmity with God" (James 4:4).

This thinking was echoed by the early church fathers.

Twenty centuries later the church finds herself institutionalized almost beyond recognition, a deeply entrenched part of the status quo. In fact its status is quite quo! I say that as a minister who loves and is committed to the institutional church. Yet I must admit that in the annals of church history God seldom, if ever, worked mightily through staid institutions. Instead, He seemed to prefer to erupt movements of correction within the institution. This is precisely what occurred in the Reformation. Now almost five hundred years later, the very groups that began as movements are themselves institutions.

Once again, in our day, there is a fresh movement of the Spirit—a fresh movement within the church. New wine is stretching old wineskins. Will they *give* or *burst?* As never before laymen are actively sharing their faith. We know now that the prophets of doom of the fifties and sixties who said the church was dying were dead wrong. There are a lot of dead churches, but there's a lot of resurrection going on, too. The church is alive and well and living in America, Europe, Africa, Asia; yes, everywhere.

The action is mainly among two groups: the traditional (noncharismatic) evangelicals and the charismatics. Often the groups overlap. This is the summer of evangelicalism and the spring of the charismatic movement! For the Christian who claims to be both evangelical and charismatic, it is a great day. Can it be that God produced the Reformation to return the church to New Testament doctrine and He is now producing the charismatic movement

38

to return the church to New Testament power? God is calling His church to more than just renewal. He is calling the church to restoration—a restoration of the dynamic and "cutting-edge" influence of the early church. In my opinion, the charismatic movement is helping to bring this about, more than any other group.

Pneumatology (the doctrine of the Holy Spirit) was dangerously underemphasized until just recently. The Bible is very clear that it is only through the power of the Holy Spirit that a believer can ever live properly as a Christian. Surely when the church underemphasizes the ministry of the Spirit, it does so to its hurt and impoverishment.

Happily, charismatics have brought the person and work of the Holy Spirit back into the limelight. Unhappily, this has sometimes, though not often, been done to the depreciation of the person and work of Christ Himself. This is just what many non-charismatics were fearful would happen. They were afraid to become involved with the charismatics for fear they might cease to be Christocentric. Their caution was sometimes legitimate.

I have seen some charismatics brush over their conversion as relatively unimportant to their baptism in the Spirit. In fairness, however, I have seen many more charismatics become beautiful witnesses to their faith in Christ, although prior to their charismatic experience they wouldn't have opened their mouths about Christ. As Clark Pinnock has said,

> An even superficial acquaintance with the movement will make sure the centrality of Christ.

39

> Honesty requires us to admit that very often there is an exuberance and joy in charismatic circles for which all believers deeply yearn.[2]

However, what has happened is that many evangelicals with a proper desire for soundness of doctrine have thrown out the baby with the bath water. They continue to be theologically sound—and powerless—while many charismatics are found wanting in theology but not in power. Must this dichotomy exist? Do we have to opt for either sound doctrine or spiritual power? Surely not. Yet in many local fellowships there seems to be no third alternative.

There has to be a third option of both New Testament doctrine and New Testament power. The times demand it. We must have a faith that gives equal honor to both the Word and the Spirit. Both are indispensable to regeneration (see John 3:6; 1 Pet. 1:23) and growth (see 2 Cor. 3:18; 2 Pet. 3:18).

Another exciting repercussion of the charismatic movement is the reemphasis on spiritual gifts. The outbreak of tongues sent many delving into their Bibles on the subject of the gifts of the Spirit. Their findings have been a most valuable asset to the church in the seventies. With some charismatic teachers stressing the importance of spiritual gifts, many noncharismatics began to study the subject also (perhaps to counter the former's teaching). For whatever reason, such notable noncharismatic Bible teachers as Ray Stedman and Bill Gothard have given much emphasis to spiritual gifts. Their insights have been well received in most quarters. But the church can thank the charismatics for bringing Body life and the ministry of spiritual gifts to the forefront.

As I stated earlier the classic Pentecostal believes that tongues is a must for experiencing the baptism or filling of the Spirit.[3] A great number of charismatics would not be quite so insistent. However, charismatics continue to make a strong case for not only the legitimacy but the desirability of tongues, as Dr. Howard M. Ervin masterfully suggests:

> But why tongues? Why not our own languages? To ask the question is to answer it. When we speak our native tongue, we speak the words that in choice, inflection, nuance and color manifest our personalities. When we speak in tongues as the Holy Spirit gives utterance, we speak those words that are the mind of the Spirit, words that manifest His personality unfettered by the censorship of the human ego. These words are, therefore, an exquisitely personal self-manifestation of the Holy Spirit."[4]

Charismatics have also made an invaluable contribution to the church in the matter of worship. It is no secret that corporate worship for many Christians is a kind of game they play. Many never get around to personal worship of God at all. It is not that way in the average Pentecostal church or charismatic conference. I have been in charismatic gatherings where the power of God was awesome. It was impossible to do anything *but* worship. True, some "get in the flesh"; they worship with such abandon that it is annoying (and even revolting) to others. But, after all, what creed says you can't lift

41

your hands and praise the Lord? The Bible says you can. It even encourages it (see 1 Tim. 2:8). What statement of faith says you can't be happy and clap your hands as you sing praises? The Bible says you can. It even warrants it (see Ps. 47:1).

The flipside is that the mature charismatic will be careful not to offend someone who is uncomfortable with such modes of worship. Here as everywhere, love must be the prevailing principle. Paul said this very thing right in the middle of his discussion on how charismatic Christians should worship in public. He said, "Though I speak with the tongues of men and of angels, and have not Charity [love], I am become as sounding brass, or a tinkling cymbal" (1 Cor. 13:1). Just as Paul gave up legitimate practices so as to not offend the weaker Christians, the charismatic should limit the more demonstrative type of worship in places where it would be deemed inappropriate.

Charismatics emphasize worship in the Spirit, that is, worship coming from the Holy Spirit. The rest of the evangelical church stresses worship based on scriptural truth. Jesus made it clear that to offer acceptable worship to God one must worship *both* in Spirit *and* in truth. They need not be exclusive. To practice true Christian worship we must make them mutually inclusive.

Sometimes, though certainly not always, charismatic worship is primarily emotional. Traditional worship, on the other hand, is primarily intellectual. Here again we have biblical precedent for both forms of worship. The Bible is replete with illustrations of highly emotional worship. For instance,

David danced before the Lord with all his might (see 2 Sam. 6:14). Jesus rejoiced greatly in His spirit (see Luke 10:21). But Jesus also sanctioned the intellectual aspect of worship when he said that the first and greatest commandment is, "Thou shalt love the Lord thy God with all thy heart, and with all thy soul, and with all thy *mind,* and with all thy strength. . ." (Mark 12:30, emphasis mine). The phrase "with all thy mind" is not found in this original command that Jesus quoted from Deuteronomy. Evidently the Lord thought intellectual worship was important enough to include it in this, the greatest commandment.

Finally, the charismatic movement is showing the church that Jesus Christ is indeed the same yesterday, today, and forever. While some Christians may question the contemporary application of James 5:14,15, charismatics simply believe it. They lay hands on the sick, pray with faith, and the sick receive healing. Charismatics claim deliverance for the demon-possessed, while most psychologists claim the whole demon business to be a holdover of medieval fantasies. And while theologians debate whether tongues still exist, charismatics just do it! They often sing the chorus:

God can do anything, anything, anything/
God can do anything but fail.

And they believe it. Along with one of their esteemed leaders, they are "expecting many miracles in the now." To charismatics, God is greater than any systematic theology that tries to stuff Him into a man-made box. In a word, charismatics really believe the triune God is *omnipotent.*

---

[1]Percy Livingston Parker, ed., *The Journal of John Wesley,* (Chicago: Moody Press, 1974), p. 239.

[2]Grant R. Osborne and Clark H. Pinnock, "A Truce Proposal for the Tongues Controversy," *Christianity Today,* Oct. 8, 1971, p. 7.

[3]See Article VII, Statement of Faith of the Assemblies of God.

[4]Howard M. Ervin, "As the Spirit Gives Utterance," *Christianity Today,* April 11, 1969, p. 11.

3

What the Noncharismatics Are Saying

Is there room in anyone's camp for someone like me? I am the son of a Pentecostal minister who feels a love and respect for the church of my roots. My seminary education is from a Southern Baptist school. I preach in many Baptist churches and I appreciate the commitment with which that denomination seeks to obey Christ's Great Commission to preach the gospel to every creature. And I have pastored an independent Bible church that stresses the importance of sound doctrine. It's a rare mix, isn't it?

I am grateful for my degree from traditional, evangelical John Brown University, and yet I am highly thankful for the contribution that Oral Roberts University has made to both of my sisters' lives. I rejoice as I see the power of God in charismatic circles, yet I am insistent that all experiences coincide with, not contradict, the Scriptures. Sometimes I feel like a man without a country.

Why do some consider it a crime to benefit from the ministries of both charismatics and noncharismatics? When will we learn that God runs the gamut of orthodox Christianity? It just could be that He's big enough to work outside our denominational context. He is God, you know. Admittedly, it can be frustrating to see God at work in circles where, in our minds, He is not supposed to be moving, but He does have the power to override our inclinations as to where and how He might function best. We had better swallow hard and accept that.

Charismatics need to understand that what they call a dry, evangelical church may not be as dead as they think. Those traditional evangelicals have some helpful doctrinal hints that sorely need to be heard and heeded by the charismatics.

There seem to be three types of evangelical church groups thriving today: those who stress evangelism, those who stress Bible study, and those who stress the gifts of the Spirit. But these three emphases need not be exclusive of each other. Are they not all intrinsic in the Great Commission as recorded in Matthew 28:19? Jesus said, "Go." That means evangelism. He said, "Teach." That means Bible training. He said, "All things." That includes the gifts of the Spirit. Therefore, are not all of these —evangelism, teaching, and the exercise of spiritual gifts—mandated for the church?[1] Without a blend of all three the church gets bloated and top heavy. A church that is all evangelism and no teaching nor gifts is denying discipleship. A church that is all teaching and no evangelism is shamefully introverted. A church that is all gifts with neither evangelism nor teaching is to be shunned.

The charismatic community must learn from the wisdom of evangelical Bible scholars other than their own. Charismatics dare not throw a person's entire ministry overboard because of a disagreement about tongues. Ministers like W. A. Criswell, Earl Radamacher, and John Walvoord should not be ignored by charismatics simply because they have strongly disagreed with the modern charismatic movement. These, too, are men of God.

Without a doubt there is much that the average charismatic can learn from the traditional evangelical Bible scholar. Not only can the charismatic learn from the scholarly message but also from the scholar's life-style and dedicated study of the Word. Charismatics meet traditional thinkers on common ground in a love for the Bible and a desire to be obedient to it. The conclusions are not the same on one subject, but so what? Look at the many areas regarding the person of Christ, salvation, and the doctrine of man where there is agreement among both groups and where charismatics can profit greatly from the research and knowledge of noncharismatic theologians. The charismatic who cannot do this has proven he is childish and carnal. First Corinthians 3:3 clearly states that it is immaturity that breeds divisions among believers. By the way, the same goes for the evangelicals who automatically turn off a charismatic Bible teacher.

A charismatic leader recently conceded that charismatics are often more dedicated to leading people into an experience of speaking in tongues than in leading them to a saving knowledge of Jesus Christ. This is a lopsided tragedy of the first order. Always in the New Testament one was filled with the Holy Spirit for the expressed purpose of being a witness—not to his experience of the filling of the Spirit—but to the saving grace of God. Jesus said,

47

"But ye shall receive power, after that the Holy Ghost is come upon you: and ye shall be witnesses unto *me* . . ." (Acts 1:8, emphasis mine).

The main message the traditional evangelical is trying to give to the charismatic is that sound doctrine is, after all, very important—far more important than our experiences.

To attempt any Christian experience without the foundation of sound doctrine is ridiculous. If the objective check of biblical doctrine is lacking, by what standard are we then to judge our spiritual experiences? The Christian life would then degenerate into a theological free-for-all. Traditional evangelicals fear that charismatics are doing precisely that.

It's worth considering. Indeed, the lack of charismatic theologians may indicate a lack of emphasis on doctrine. There are hundreds of "Bible teachers" but few charismatic theologians in the proper and best sense of that word.

In fairness, however, this may be because the charismatic movement is still relatively young. Also, there *are* a few gifted charismatic scholars who will probably make valuable contributions to Christian thought in the years ahead. However, a comprehensive charismatic theology has yet to be developed.

Traditional evangelicals are also concerned over the apparent noncommitment of some charismatics to the local church. I have heard several evangelicals say that, whatever else the baptism in the Spirit may make of charismatics, it makes them "church-hoppers." That kind of blanket statement is unwarranted. But clearly this is a problem for too many charismatics.

My personal theory as to why this problem exists is that newly baptized-in-the-Spirit charismatics sincerely desire to follow God's Spirit. So some follow Him from church to church! Maturity should teach this dear brother or sister that God the Spirit is omnipresent. He's in churches all over town at the same time! There's no way you can see what's happening everywhere in a given city on a given Sunday morning at eleven o'clock.

Frankly I am disturbed by *any* Christians who neglect their personal lives before God and their commitment to a local body of believers. With no offense intended, I say that no one has any business at a "deeper life" conference who hasn't mastered the basics of a daily devotional life, consistent personal witness, and loyal involvement in a local biblically orthodox church.

One reason why the "shepherding" controversy has been so widespread is that the need for a loving, caring fellowship is vital to any Christian. Consequently if one has no deacons, elders, or pastor, "shepherds" must be invented. Since the Christian who skips from church to church lacks the small group dynamics of Sunday school, he must get into a "discipleship group." I am not insinuating that discipleship groups are bad. On the contrary. But I am saying that they are to be part of, not separate from, the local church body.

Perhaps the most biting accusation against charismatics is that they tend to split churches. Actually, the criticism cuts both ways. The trouble comes when charismatics try to pressure their form of worship upon the whole church body, or when noncharismatics try to repress spiritual gifts. Dear charismatic brother or sister, please read carefully.

God has not commissioned you to preach the gospel of "the baptism." He has commissioned you to preach the gospel of salvation in Jesus Christ! Non-charismatic friend, don't reject Christians who have gifts that you don't understand. Remember that the Holy Spirit "apportions to each one individually as he wills" (1 Cor. 12:11, RSV), and His gifts are for the good of all.

A wise charismatic brother jokingly said to me, "Everything would be okay if we could lock a guy up for six months right after he receives the baptism." It is often in that initial six months after the experience, when he has a new power he doesn't quite know how to handle, that the new charismatic may do or say something indiscreet.

Recently I tried to rehearse every embarrassing situation in my life. Inevitably, they all began when *I said something foolish.* James describes it plainly:

> For in many things we offend all. If any man offend not in word, the same is a perfect man, and able also to bridle the whole body. Behold, we put bits in the horses' mouths, that they may obey us; and we turn about the whole body. Behold also the ships, which though they be great, and are driven of fierce winds, yet are they turned about with a very small helm, whithersoever the governor listeth. Even so the tongue is a little member, and boasteth great things. Behold how great a matter a little fire kindleth! (James 3:2–5).

Charismatic, strive to strike a balance. The Christian life is the Christ-life. There is much more to the Holy Spirit's ministry than gifts. He also indwells, seals, empowers, and produces fruit in the believer. If we are going to talk about the Holy Spirit—and certainly we should—let's talk about *all* that He's doing in the world today.

Because many charismatics often are experience oriented, one day thousands of disgruntled charismatics may wake up and ask, "Is that all there is?" The happy answer is no. That is by no means all there is in the economy and plan of God for you. The baptism or filling of the Holy Spirit is not the end. It is the means to an end—Christlikeness. And Christlikeness is not a singular experience; it is a lifelong journey. Not only are we to be filled with the Spirit, we are to walk in the Spirit. And walking takes time.

Let me suggest that all of us, traditional evangelicals and charismatics alike, talk too much about speaking in tongues. Speaking in tongues is mentioned specifically in seven chapters in the Bible, but there are 1,189 chapters in the Bible. That means that even if they do disagree on tongues, there are 1,182 chapters forming the basis for potential fellowship between noncharismatics and charismatics.

------

[1]Actually, the only imperative command in Matthew 28:19,20 is μαθητεύσατε, "make disciples." The other verbs are Greek participles modifying the imperative command.

4

Leaven in the Charismatic Lump

Some charismatics give the impression that they are always joyful, always victorious, and always living above their problems. Such, however, is not the case. No one, charismatic or not, bats one thousand in Christian living. As a matter of fact, it is often a stark, unhappy realization to new initiates into the movement that baptism in the Spirit does not deliver them from their problems, nor does it deliver them from their immaturity.

It has been my impression that the baptism in the Holy Spirit (as charismatics define it) produces different results in different people. Invariably it does produce joy. It often produces more boldness in witness for Christ. For many it is a major step toward Christian maturity. But for others who are untaught and undisciplined it can actually become a step backward. Permit me to offer some specific counsel for charismatics who are having trouble.

Let's aim for steadiness. Often charismatics are spiritual sprinters, great in the one-hundred-yard dash but poor marathon runners in the lifelong race that is set before us.

Sometimes charismatics are victimized by incoherence and an aimless drifting in their Christian life. (However, aimlessness is not unique to charismatics!) In advanced cases of this severe spiritual myopia, one actually becomes addicted to experiences. The result is, like any addict, he must receive larger doses to maintain the desired effect. Thus it is not uncommon for some charismatics to have a very brief span of loyalty to their teachers and pastors. When a man and his ministry can no longer produce the thrill that was once experienced, these misguided ones seek a "deeper walk" through a new ministry.

Let's all get back to objective truth. One of the great expressions of pseudo-Christianity in our day is sensualism. By that I do not mean sexual sensuality. I simply mean the desire in our generation to *feel*. As never before, we relate feeling to knowing. Our generation operates on the assumption that feeling produces knowing—a complete reversal of the traditional concept that knowing produces feeling. The Eastern religious cults, like Hare Krishna and TM, are prime examples of the idea that sensations produce knowledge.

The increased interest in the sensual partially explains why sex gets dirtier and crime gets more violent in the entertainment media. As our senses are dulled to the more mundane prime-time grime, we open up to more high-powered stimuli. So it is in religion as well. I believe that the charismatic movement found such an open audience among the Jesus People in the early part of this decade because young people have a great desire to integrate feeling and faith.

There is, of course, nothing wrong with this desire. Our Christian faith is and ought to be heartfelt.

54

But feelings should by no stretch of the imagination be the basis for our faith. That's playing the Hindu game. The Christian faith is based on objective historical data concerning the person and work of the Lord Jesus Christ. When that foundation is replaced with another, the whole structure begins to crumble. Again let me point out that many different evangelicals—not just charismatics—have succumbed to this tendency.

There is, then, a great problem in the desire for sensual worship at any cost. Since many in the charismatic movement who are less mature are either unable or unwilling to "try the spirits [as to] whether they are of God" (1 John 4:1), they are wide open to deception, which at best can be an emotional counterfeit and at worst a demonic one.

Let's agree to follow Christ, even in the absence of feelings. There is a danger that the craving for experience will keep you from the disciplines of Christian growth that are less exciting. It is not always a thrill to study the Bible. Sometimes the obedient Christian must verbalize his faith simply out of sheer obedience to the Great Commission given by our Lord. Often true prayer is anything but fun. Intercessory prayer can be a combat with the prince of the power of the air. Jesus sweat drops of blood when he prayed. Paul travailed in prayer. The great saints of God through the ages have agonized as prayer warriors. In short, Christian growth is not all fun and games.

Jesus described discipleship as taking up a cross. The cross is always an instrument for dying. To live as Christ would have us to live and to mature into His image, we must experience what He experienced—death. Paul said in Galatians 2:20, "I am crucified with Christ: nevertheless I live; yet not I, but Christ liveth in me: and the life which I now live in the flesh I live by the faith of the Son of God who loved me and gave himself for me." It is a tragic truth among too many Christians that the vital, necessary ingredients of deep prayer and study of the Scriptures are sacrificed on the altar of immediate sensual enjoyment.

You may have great spiritual gifts, but if you do not undergo the spiritual disciplines of prayer and study of the Word you will be a malformed babe in Christ with gifts you don't know how to handle. If that happens, you will be in the same class as the Corinthian believers, who though spiritually gifted were desperately carnal.

Often the plain fact is that the gifts of the Spirit operate in lives that are shallow and lacking in the fruit of the Spirit. In this, there is a sovereignty of God that I do not fully understand. Evidently the bestowal of spiritual gifts is just as much a result of grace as is our salvation. Still the messenger sometimes cancels out the message. The package sometimes depreciates the gift.

It's important, too, that we make sure our authority structures are biblical. A great strength and at the same time a great weakness of the charismatic movement is its loose structure. This has provided opportunity for a spontaneity that has spawned great growth and a feeling of freedom and liberty within charismatic circles.

People today want less structure, less of the "this is the way it has to be done" attitude. However, many have discovered the obvious: People cannot live without some system of authority.

A few charismatics who are not strong participants in local churches have formed shepherd groups. They have traded the biblical formula of church administration for an unscriptural one that rivals the worst imperialism of pre-Reformation Roman Catholicism. These, of course, are extreme and relatively rare occurrences, but they are happening. The "shepherd" may decide whether one should go to the dentist, have a vacation, change jobs, or do a thousand other things ranging from minutiae to extremely important decisions. In some cases, the doctrine of the priesthood of all believers is washed down the drain, and in its place an unsound substitute for free will is inaugurated. This, indeed, is unholy leaven in the charismatic lump.

While charismatics are not exempt from problems, neither are they strangers to great potential. If we can view the next ten years of the church with any accuracy at all, the future seems to belong to the charismatics. Glossolalia is here to stay.

Let's be careful how we use terminology. Glossolalia is a word derived from two Greek words: *glossa* meaning the tongue and *laleo* or *lalia* meaning to speak. So a glossolalist is one who speaks in tongues. Gratefully, more and more Christians are willing to accept this obviously biblical gift as a valid occurrence that is available to Christians today through the sovereign bestowal of the Holy Spirit.

What many outside the charismatic groups are not ready to accept is the inference that only those who speak in tongues are "Spirit-filled." More than once I have heard the silly statement that Billy Graham or another godly noncharismatic was "used of the Spirit" or "led of the Spirit" or even "full of the Spirit" but not filled with the Spirit! The only basis given for this unwarranted claim is the fact that the noncharismatic has not spoken in tongues. Such a statement is by no means characteristic of the entire charismatic movement; nevertheless, many charismatics equate being filled with the Spirit with a "once upon a time" experience of speaking in tongues. There is little question as to other Christians' fruit, love, or effectiveness of ministry. The only big question seems to be: "Did they speak in tongues?"

So let's be careful how we use terms. This exclusive usage of the term "Spirit-filled" to include only charismatics is grievous to traditional evangelicals. If only those who speak in tongues are filled with the Spirit, then Luther, Calvin, Wesley, Whitfield, Edwards, Spurgeon, Moody, Torrey, Sunday, and Graham must never have been filled with the Spirit! That is pure absurdity!

Another red-flag term employed by both the new charismatics and classic Pentecostals is the term "full gospel." The rationale for use of the term is that the charismatic or Pentecostal church presents Christ not only as Savior and Lord but also as Healer and Baptizer in the Holy Spirit. The inference is that all churches that are not charismatic or Pentecostal are "half gospel" or "part gospel." One can understand the dismay this arouses among many traditional evangelicals who have given their lives to a defense of the gospel.

Paul described the gospel that he preached in 1 Corinthians 15:1–4:

> Moreover, brethren, I declare unto you the gospel which I preached unto you . . . . For I delivered unto you first of all that which I also received, how that Christ died for our sins according to the scriptures; And that he was buried, and that he rose again the third day according to the scriptures . . . .

Any church, then, that preaches what Paul preached is a full gospel church. That *is* the full gospel: Christ died for our sins and rose again. This is the Good News that we are to declare to the world. So all of us should be more judicious in our use of terms like "Spirit-filled" and "full gospel."

Let's make our basis for fellowship a common faith. We need to ask ourselves: Are we united by common faith or by common experience? Experience can be quite misleading. But belief in objective data is a far more solid basis for fellowship. For two thousand years Christians have been bound together by a common *faith* in Christ and by belief in the historical evidence about Him recorded in the Gospels. Christians are *not* of one body because of a common *experience* in Christ. It is important that we all understand this. True, we have all had an experience of being saved by grace through faith. But our experiences of conversion vary greatly. So our faith must be in the objective revelation of God's written Word. Whenever it is otherwise we open ourselves to deception and, yes, heresy.

If common experience is placed as a higher motif for fellowship than common faith, we have opened the door to all kinds of false doctrine. My own experiences have varied, but my faith in Jesus Christ and in His Word has remained constant through the last twenty-five years, in spite of extremely differing situations and circumstances. The basis for Christian fellowship is common faith, not common experience.

Finally, let's get a biblical definition of what it means to be spiritual. I am unhappy with the attitude of super-spirituality that is sometimes expressed among charismatics. The impression seems to be, "I have something you don't have. I know what my Christian life was like before I had the baptism, and I know what it's like now. Therefore, since you have not had this experience, you must be living the kind of substandard Christian life I was living before the baptism." Such an inference is prejudicial and, of course, often false. Furthermore, spiritual pride is not from God.

Charismatics rightly believe that one must be filled with the Holy Spirit to live a life pleasing to God. But they are wrong to believe that all experiences of the baptism or filling must be measured by the occurrences they deem important. Even a cursory reading of the Book of Acts will reveal that when the Holy Spirit fell on different people and groups the accompanying experiences were beautifully diverse.

5

On the Other Hand . . .

In the last chapter, I mentioned that some charismatics imply they are part of a super-spiritual elite simply because they speak in tongues. It is equally true, however, that many non-charismatics believe they are super-spiritual simply because they do *not* speak in tongues. They feel they have been "wise as serpents" and have escaped this terrible "false doctrine" of modern "tongues speaking" (as they often refer to it).

Earlier I said the mud-slinging battle was tied. But if I had to give the edge to one of these two groups, I would have to give that dubious award to the noncharismatic community, especially the conservative evangelicals.

Even the more tolerant traditionalists say charismatics should display "more balance" in their lives and witness. Yet for all the talk on "balanced Christian living" among evangelicals, I see very little balance. We catch hold of a spiritual truth and make it our watchword. Suddenly our message becomes "faith" or "confession" or "submission" or "discipleship" or "the Word" or "prayer." We can even become unbalanced by always harping about "balance"! All of these truths are legitimate, wonderful, and biblical, but *none* of them is to be the thrust of our message. Our message is Jesus! If we are not constantly looking to Him, our "balance," our spiritual equilibrium, will eventually be shot. We achieve balance only as we steadfastly gaze upon Him, and when we do, all of these other teachings fall into their proper places. It is an insidious flaw of fallen human nature that we want to emphasize gifts instead of the Giver, miracles instead of the Miracle-Worker, truth instead of *the* Truth, Christians instead of Christ. We have probably all been guilty of improper emphasis at some point.

Charismatics have often been faulted by traditional evangelicals for being unconcerned about the lost. This is simply not true. In many countries, in fact throughout South America, the Pentecostals are leading the way in missionary activity. Such has been the confession of evangelicals like Stan Mooneyham and C. Peter Wagner. In our own country charismatics now may be outdistancing even the Baptists in evangelistic endeavors.

Though they sometimes may stress the wrong things, it is completely unfair to say that charismatics are not evangelistic. The traditional evangelical should take a cold, hard look at the church today in the Western world. He will not be happy with what he sees. There is little power, and few take evangelism seriously. And, quite frankly, an objective view will reveal that the charismatic movement is just about the only thing that even looks like a heaven-sent spiritual awakening in the church.

There are many evangelicals who are rejoicing at the sound of abundance of rain, even if the cloud formations do look charismatic. Certainly not all of the traditional evangelicals are intolerant of charismatics. But many noncharismatics, even those we would expect to be much kinder and wiser, have made incredibly rash statements. I sat in disbelief and grief as I heard a gifted evangelist say, "This tongues thing is ninety-five percent of the devil." Now I'd say that's just a little steep! A famous southern pastor chalked it up as "just a women's movement." I find a statement like that amazing for one who is usually so careful in his speech.

Of course there are satanic counterfeits in (actually on the fringes of) the charismatic movement. But there are also satanic counterfeits among other evangelicals. Traditional evangelicals have had their share of Elmer Gantrys too. But that only demonstrates the validity of what is happening. You cannot have a counterfeit without its opposite. Many Christians do have the real thing; and if their gifts are from Satan, then he has made a big mistake, because most who receive a spiritual gift afterwards display an ardent love for the Lord Jesus.

There is always the tendency, as some have done, to throw a blanket indictment over the charismatic movement. This is much easier than it is to obey the scriptural injunction to "try the spirits whether they are of God" (1 John 4:1). Each occurrence of spiritual gifts should be tried separately under the spotlight of God's Word. I am convinced that sheer total obedience to 1 Corinthians 12–14 would solve all, I repeat *all,* of the problems regarding spiritual gifts. Those experiences that conform to biblical patterns should be gratefully accepted. Those which do not should be rejected. It's as simple as that.

63

Indeed, the greatest need of the church right now is the gift of discernment. We should ask God to give each local church men and women who can discern the true force behind each supposed manifestation of God. It grieves me that so many people are asking the Holy Spirit for the gift of tongues when a much more needed gift for the church today is the discerning of spirits. Spiritual manifestations can emanate from any one of three sources: the devil, the flesh, or the Holy Spirit. How desperately we need those who can discern the sources of the myriad of manifestations among believers today!

A couple of red-flag terms that charismatics often use were mentioned in the last chapter. Noncharismatics also use a red-flag term: "tongues movement." This label is narrow and unfair. There is far more to the charismatic movement than what meets the tongue! Lifeless Christians have been turned into joyful, loving disciples of the Lord. Indeed, there is an exuberance among charismatics that is almost entirely missing in the rest of the body of Christ. Some of the boldest and most exciting evangelistic ventures of our time are being undertaken by charismatics. A sensitivity to human suffering, especially physical, is far more evidenced among charismatics than among other evangelicals. In short, it is just not fair to call it a tongues movement. It is not a tongues movement—it is a charismatic movement. The message of this movement to the church is a reemphasis on *all* the gifts of the Holy Spirit.

Yet there are those who fear this movement like the plague. I know some dear pastor friends who are scared to death there will be an outbreak of "tongues" in their church. They hear horrifying stories of how charismatics have split other churches, and these pastors live out their days in mortal fear that the same thing will happen in their churches. As a result they often take a hard-line stand against the charismatic movement and preach against it with loud words and weak exegesis.

Pastor, the best way to insure an outbreak of tongues in your church is to preach against it! Your people will be so curious they will read every book they can get their hands on and talk to every charismatic they know. How much better it would be to adopt the position held by A. B. Simpson, the founder of the Christian and Missionary Alliance, who was by no means a charismatic. "The attitude," he said, "of tongues held by pastor and people should be, 'Seek not, forbid not.'" Or, as United Presbyterian pastor Jerry Kirk of Cincinnati said not long ago, "Here at College Hill Presbyterian Church we *encourage* all the gifts of the Spirit; however, we do not *emphasize* gifts of the Spirit."

6

Love Shed Abroad

Some time ago I was privileged to attend the School of the Prophets at the great First Baptist Church of Dallas. The leadership of this church has persistently insisted that the charismatic position is an improper interpretation of the biblical teaching on spiritual gifts. Believe it or not, Charismatic, the Holy Spirit mightily ministered to me that week through the people and pastor of that wonderful church.

The next Sunday I attended the exciting Beverly Hills Baptist Church in Dallas. This church has grown from a few hundred to a few thousand in just a short time since the outbreak of the charismatic movement within that church. Believe it or not, Traditional Evangelical, the Holy Spirit ministered to me equally through that church and its pastor.

As I thought on the edification I had received in both churches, I mused that there were probably members in both of those dear fellowships who think that it is impossible for the Holy Spirit to be genuinely at work in the other church! When I sat in the great sanctuary of the First Baptist Church and listened to the marvelous music and great preaching, I thought how wonderful it would be if some of

67

the Beverly Hills spontaneity could be added to this already grand worship experience. And while I participated in the worship at Beverly Hills I thought how wonderful it would be if this church fellowship had a little more decorum and some of the strong disciples that are so prevalent at the downtown First Church.

The point is: We need each other! I cannot in good conscience sing that part of the verse of "Onward Christian Soldiers" that says, "We are not divided/ All one body we." It's as plain as the nose on your face that we are divided. We are fractured into thousands of pieces, resulting in a weak and soft witness for Christ. This is not to say we should become crusading proponents of unity at any cost. But Christians could do a far better job of conveying spiritual unity and still maintain their denominational distinctives.

Traditional evangelicals emphasize the preaching and teaching of the Word of God. The more liberal denominations, at least in the past few decades, have tended to have a keener social awareness. Charismatics give heavy emphasis to the power of the Holy Spirit. But note the blend of all three in the style of Paul's ministry: "For I will not dare to speak of any of those things which Christ hath not wrought by me, to make the Gentiles obedient, by word and deed, through mighty signs and wonders, by the power of the Spirit of God . . ." (Rom. 15:18,19). Paul speaks here of three aspects of his ministry. Evidently he gave equal emphasis to each: (1) the Word, (2) deeds, and (3) the power of the Spirit. These three aspects of Paul's ministry correspond exactly to these three branches of Christendom today. The Word is stressed among evangelicals. Good deeds are stressed by the more liberal denominations. The power of the Spirit is stressed among Pentecostals and charismatics.

Is it impossible to dream of a church fellowship that places equal emphasis on all three aspects of ministry? Not really. For if all of the gifts of the Holy Spirit were in operation, with the manifestations of the fruit of the Spirit, there would be absolutely no lack, not only in the church universal but also in any local body of believers. Yet many churches resist the gifts of the Spirit fearing dissension. But let's call this fear what it is—it's quenching the Spirit. God has not given us the spirit of fear.

It is true that charismatic occurrences sometimes disrupt the harmony that should exist in the body of Christ. The noncharismatic is agitated and the charismatic becomes defensive or vice versa. And yet the Bible says in Romans 5:5, ". . . the love of God is shed abroad in our hearts by the Holy Ghost which is given unto us." Only one thing is proved when charismatics and noncharismatics fight each other about the gifts of the Spirit: Neither group is filled with the Spirit! I would like to suggest to both charismatics and noncharismatics that the *real* evidence of the filling of the Holy Spirit is that the love of God is shed abroad in our hearts. To be filled with the Spirit is to be filled with God. John said, "God is love" (John 4:8). Therefore to be filled with the Spirit is to be filled with love.

The sound doctrine of a loveless traditional evangelical stinks just as badly as the dead orthodoxy of the Pharisee. The loveless charismatic may have his gifts, but he is as pitifully carnal as the baby Christians at Corinth.

"Though I speak with the tongues of men and of angels, and have not charity [love], I am become as sounding brass, or a tinkling cymbal." (1 Cor. 13:1). At Corinth in Paul's day, worship of pagan gods was common. The spirits of these false gods were beckoned by the loud clashing of cymbals. In 1 Corinthians 13:1 Paul is really saying that if spiritual gifts (here he particularly mentions tongues) are not accompanied by love, it is no better than pagan worship! So I want to go on record as stating that the Holy Spirit has never been responsible for even one church split. Never! This is because agápe love, the very love of God, is shed abroad in our hearts by the Holy Spirit (see Rom. 5:5).

Some Christians are afflicted with charismania (an obsession with spiritual gifts). Others are ill with charisphobia (a fear of spiritual gifts). We should neither be charismaniacs nor charisphobiacs. We should be truly charismatic, in the highest biblical sense of the word, joyfully exercising the gift or gifts that the Holy Spirit has graciously given to us.

Right now I'm thinking of two Christian organizations, both of which are marvelously used of God. One of these organizations refuses to accept people who speak in tongues because they fear the issue will be divisive to their interdenominational structure. The other group will not accept those who do not speak in tongues, feeling that only those who speak with tongues are anointed of the Holy Spirit and that their ministry requires Spirit-filled men and women. I respect the right of both groups to form whatever policies they feel led to form under God. But let me suggest that the one organization is too inhibitive and the other organization is too exclusive, and that both organizations are wrong. These organizational policies are simply illustrative of the fear and distrust that is often present in both camps against the other group.

One of my sisters spent her freshman year in college at John Brown University, a traditional evangelical institution. At the end of that year she felt led of the Lord to transfer to Oral Roberts University, a charismatic institution. Several of her friends at J.B.U. were, to say the least, surprised; they wondered what a girl like her would do in a place like that. They couldn't believe that one could be both grounded in the Word and charismatic.

Just this morning I heard a fine evangelist deliberately misrepresent the charismatic movement to a Bible study group. This afternoon he left for another series of meetings to preach about the love of God.

A friend of mine told me that at the charismatic Bible college he attended the students would group together and discuss how liberal certain Southern Baptist seminaries are, giving the impression that all Southern Baptists are rank liberals who deny miracles and the Word of God. I even heard a Pentecostal preacher say that Baptists don't believe in the Holy Spirit! That's quite an accusation to aim against such an evangelistic group. It is the Holy Spirit, afterall, who is at work when people are drawn to Christ. On that basis—the basis of the ministry of the Spirit in bringing people to Christ—

71

it would be interesting to see which group believes more fully in the power of the Holy Spirit.

These are just a few of many incidents where people jump to unfortunate conclusions because of (1) a predisposition against the "other side," and (2) misinformation or the lack of information, and (3) faulty analysis of the isolated facts they do have. Christian, get the big picture before you draw any conclusions. A good rule for living is: Before you speak, get the whole story.

It has been my observation, after studying this subject and listening to both groups for several years, that most derogatory statements made by members of either group are made from misinformation or from insufficient information. And this is dangerous by any standard. Jesus warns that we will be brought into judgment for "every idle word." I feel certain that both charismatics and non-charismatics will have a lot of idle words about each other to "fess up to" when they stand before the Lord.

But how about this for a breath of fresh air? Some time back I sat in a great denominational rally and heard the speaker say, "From my hotel room in a great city in Brazil I could hear the Pentecostal preacher proclaiming to the crowds, 'Cristo! Cristo! Cristo!' I tell you, if our denomination doesn't evangelize Brazil the Pentecostals will!"

I was sitting next to a pastor from this denomination. He turned to me and said, "If we have the money and they have the message, let's just give our money to the Pentecostals and let them keep doing the job." How beautiful and how needed is that kind of bridge across the evangelical troubled waters.

7

A Warning to Charismatics

I have approached the writing of this chapter with a good deal of trepidation. I sense the possibility of being misunderstood and/or misquoted. However I must say what is on my heart. I have prayed over every word. If these things are not said there can never be a charismatic truce. The things I will expose in this chapter are the hidden questions of thousands of conservative evangelicals. I approach them and offer some warnings only after years of observation and prayer concerning the corporate situation among charismatics.

The first warning I give to charismatics is the warning against deception. Much has been said already about the deceptiveness of highly sensuous religious experiences. By the end of this decade I believe there will be miracles all over the place: miracles from heaven and miracles from hell. Since charismatics have a strong orientation toward the supernatural, the devil will try to delude them so that they will believe a lie. It wouldn't be the first time. After the great revival in Wales during the early years of this century, there was a nightmarish aftermath.[1] Thousands of sincere Christians were caught up in demonic counterfeits because they craved the supernatural. It could happen again. In fact, in some cases, it is already happening.

Glossolalia is not uniquely Christian. It is also found among pagans, Hindus, Mormons, and others. Some converts from the drug culture say that tongues was part of their psychedelic experience. It is a sheer disaster to accept any expression of tongues without any attempt at discernment in this vital area. There are false manifestations. There are true manifestations. Happy is the Christian who is always right in knowing which are the true appearances and which are the false.

Many have mistakenly believed that the baptism in the Holy Spirit is a shortcut to spiritual maturity. But why not? After all, this is the instant generation. We're programmed for instant answers. The most complex mysteries can be solved in a one-hour TV drama. We have instant coffee, instant tea, instant dinners, instant relief. Why not instant spirituality? Simply because there is no such thing. God doesn't work that way. Almost always the work of the Holy Spirit is a slow, hot work. Far from being a shortcut to maturity, the baptism in the Spirit is simply a gateway into an adventure of Christian growth. The baptism in the Spirit is a means to an end (conformity to Christ), but certainly it is not an end in itself.

At this point the experience of the Corinthian Christians is a solemn warning to us. It is obvious from Paul's first epistle that they had been baptized with the Holy Spirit (see 1 Cor. 12:13). They also were endowed with all spiritual gifts (see 1 Cor. 1:4–7). Even so Paul rebukes them as unspiritual people. He points out that the evidence of the

Spirit's fullness is not the exercise of gifts but the ripening of fruit. He could not write to them "as unto spiritual, but as unto carnal, even as unto babes in Christ" (1 Cor. 3:1).

Sooner or later every Christian sees that the attaining of the goal of Christlikeness is a life-long process. But for those who are deceived by false teaching on this matter early in their Christian life the truth can be very disheartening and disillusioning. As my old English professor used to say, "Man learns too late to be wise." Again I predict that there well may be a whole generation of disillusioned charismatics who will find out that they have to go through the same hard experiences as every other Christian believer to reach maturity in Christ. In fact, this disillusionment and disenchantment has already happened to hundreds of former Jesus People who were "high on Jesus" but never deeply into the Word.

As a former pastor I was meticulous about who received the privilege of speaking to the congregation over which God had placed me. Therefore, I am not just a little concerned by the seemingly flippant attitude on the part of charismatic pastors and conference directors who have only one criterion for their speakers: speaking in tongues. It matters not that the speaker may come from a liberal church background and in fact be quite liberal in theology. The only question seems to be, "Do we have a common experience?"

A person who denies such cardinal doctrines as blood atonement, the bodily resurrection of Christ, and a literal heaven and hell is not welcome in my pulpit! In fairness it should be said that most liberal churchmen who receive a charismatic experience become more conservative theologically as a result. But this is not always true; and if a person's doctrine is defective, no amount of spiritual gifts will sanctify the impure doctrine. The baptism in the Holy Spirit cannot serve as a cover for heterodox belief.

There is a yet more subtle potential heresy for many charismatics—worship of experiences rather than worship of the God of the experiences. To have a great spiritual encounter and then to become enamored with the experience rather than with the Lord Himself is sophisticated idolatry. We are not to exalt the gift but the Giver. We are not to go out to praise the gift or experience but rather ". . . to shew forth the praises of him who hath called you out of darkness into his marvellous light" (1 Pet. 2:9). Creeds, prayers, nature, the Bible, gifts of grace; these are not to be worshiped in themselves. They are vehicles of worshiping and serving God. As the famous song says, "Beyond the sacred page I seek Thee, Lord."

No Christian would ever think of willfully disobeying the first commandment, "Thou shalt have no other gods before Me." But sometimes the trappings of Christianity take the place of Christ Himself. We must be alert, lest we find ourselves at the foot—not of the Cross—but of the golden calf.

One of the "must believe" doctrines of Christian orthodoxy is justification by faith. If we are ever to be declared righteous in God's sight, it will clearly be by our faith in Christ's completed work at Calvary for us and "*not* by works of righteousness which we have done" (see Titus 3:5).

Many traditional evangelicals hesitate to endorse the charismatic movement because of the strange bedfellows among charismatics. It is undeniable that the vast majority of charismatics are evangelical; that is, they do believe that a person is saved by placing his faith in Christ alone. However, many traditional evangelicals question (legitimately, I believe) why some evangelical charismatics do not disassociate themselves from church communions that deny justification by faith alone. If they stay in their heterodox church to be a witness for Christ, that is one thing. But if they stay there because they actually espouse the position of their church that salvation can be accomplished by some method other than simple faith in Christ, that is quite another. In such a case, they have never been truly born again. And anyone who speaks in tongues but has not been born again is manifesting not a spiritual gift but a spiritual counterfeit.

Evangelicals have historically been cautious regarding church unions involving several different denominations. They realize that an ecumenical spirit based on theological inclusiveness could create a conducive climate in which to spawn a diabolical one-world church. Thus, they have a built-in hesitancy about almost anything that has an interchurch flavor.

However, there is a true ecumenism and a false. True ecumenicity is based primarily on unity in the Spirit, which should manifest itself visibly before the unbelieving world. Certainly there is much of this evident among charismatics. Without a doubt God is drawing His true church, made up of all who trust in Christ alone to save them, together. A fresh, sweet spirit of cooperation and love is evident among many Christians from diverse backgrounds.

But there is another ecumenism that is not so wholesome. This ecumenical movement is more structured. What it lacks in biblical theology it tries to make up for in a broad-based, peace-at-any-price theological pluralism.

Some traditional evangelicals believe that too many charismatics willingly embrace all who have spoken in tongues, no matter how weak their theology may be. Indeed, *Christian Life* magazine reported that charismatics generally are not too interested in theology. If this is true, it is a chilling example of the potential for pseudo-Christian unions based not on oneness of faith nor even oneness of the Spirit but on sincerity of common experiences.

An experience with God's Spirit should lead us out of error and into truth. As Jesus said, "When he, the Spirit of truth is come, he will guide you into all truth ..." (John 16:13). The doctrinal differences between evangelical churches and some other communions represented in the charismatic movement are immense. They cannot and should not be glossed over simply by pointing to the common experience of salvation or baptism in the Spirit that some from both groups may share.

The current "prosperity" kick of some charismatics also disturbs me. I recently listened to several charismatic preachers who came back to back on a Christian radio station. Invariably their message was the same: financial prosperity.

Most of those preachers came from poor, rural

backgrounds, and now God has blessed them finan-cially. But I don't appreciate their tricking their listeners into believing that God wants *everybody* to be fabulously wealthy or that wealth begins by exercising faith and sending a generous offering to their ministry.

Try telling the suffering Christians in India, Rus-sia, or Uganda that it is God's will for them to be rich and that the only reason they aren't is their lack of faith! If it is a spiritual deficiency that makes and keeps one poor, we might well ask what the defi-ciency was in the life of Jesus, or Paul, or Saint Francis of Assisi, or countless other godly believers. It is true that God will supply all our needs. It is true that God doesn't desire that His children be in want. It is *not* true that God wants all of His children to be materially wealthy.

In a time when there is massive financial instabil-ity, many Christians are choosing to place their faith in—of all things—the deceitfulness of riches. Old time Pentecostals measured divine favor by the strength of their piety. Are today's charismatics measuring divine favor by the strength of their bank accounts?

This leads us to a final warning: In too many instances the life-style of charismatics betrays their testimony of being filled or baptized with the Spirit. A notable Pentecostal, Donald Gee, spoke to this matter when he said, "There is something radically wrong with the experience that gives you gifts and doesn't give you holiness. Some baptisms are disap-pointing because some people have been urged to speak in what *seemed* to be tongues, and I doubt if they really have had the baptism at all."[2]

Some sections of Christendom are referred to as the "holiness" movement. This is something of a misnomer. The whole Christian church should be a holiness movement! Christians are called unto holiness. Our lives are to be a sharp contrast and rebuke to the intemperate indulgences of unbelievers.

Practical holiness comes hard. It is not achieved by a once-upon-a-time filling of the Spirit. Rather, it is the result of a day by day walk in the Spirit and denial of the lusts of the flesh. Such a life will produce, in the Puritan's term, "gospel holiness."

If these issues are not dealt with in a forthright manner, a charismatic truce is unthinkable. I have not raised these points to agitate. Rather, I am interested in fostering *true* unity in the body of Christ. After all, this is a major goal of the church: "Till we all come in the unity of the faith . . ." (Eph. 4:13). But we must understand that it is a unity of *faith,* not experience.

---

[1]See *War On The Saints* by Jessie Penn-Lewis in collaboration with Evan Roberts (Christian Literature Crusade: Fort Washington, Pennsylvania), n. d.

[2]Harold Lindsell, "Tests for the Tongues Movement," *Christianity Today,* 1972, p. 2.

8

A Warning to Noncharismatics

The Holy Spirit is God. Therefore, He is a person. He can be grieved, quenched, and blasphemed. Some traditional evangelicals, it seems to me, have come dangerously close to doing all three. The context of Ephesians 4:30 makes it obvious that to grieve the Holy Spirit is to be guilty of conduct unbecoming of a Christian. To quench the Holy Spirit is, in effect, to try to tie His hands by written or unwritten standards of conduct for Him in our lives and worship experiences, both personal and corporate. In the context of Jesus' discussion of blaspheming the Holy Spirit in Mark 3:20–30, it is clear that to blaspheme the Holy Spirit is not only to give a final rejection to Jesus Christ as Savior but also to attribute the works of the Holy Spirit to Satan. Although I do not believe that a Christian can blaspheme the Holy Spirit, I have watched with alarm as many evangelicals most readily and flippantly have accused the entire charismatic movement of being a work of the devil. Draw your own conclusions. On this issue I urge all noncharismatics to be more careful before they speak. It is one thing to say that the charismatic movement is in error. It is certainly another to say that it is from the devil!

It's evident that traditional evangelicals have produced very gifted Bible teachers. However, several wonderful evangelical teachers from whom I have profited immensely intrigue me at the point of their teaching on the gifts of the Spirit. I have never seen them stretch so far nor so hard as in their attempt to explain away certain gifts of the Spirit. Their intricate, obscure formulas for arriving at the conclusion that certain gifts have ceased is, at times, almost comical. To me, it is Exhibit A of some of the poorest exegesis, born out of bias, to be found anywhere in Christendom.

It is ironic that the traditional evangelical, who places so much emphasis on objective truth, on this issue tries to decide *subjectively* which gifts of the Spirit have ceased and which ones are still operating! You can't smorgasboard the gifts of the Spirit.

Even if it could be proved (which it cannot) that some of the gifts of the Spirit were withdrawn at the end of the apostolic era, we could not conclude that the Spirit is not able to bestow them again for such an hour as this. The traditional evangelical teacher certainly has no teaching from Scripture that proves that any spiritual gift would cease to function in this period of the church. So he must try to pick for himself which gifts are valid and which are not. We dare not try to bind God's hands with a questionable theological theory. How dare we try to deny God the right to bestow gifts to His church!

It is sometimes argued by traditional evangelicals that charismatics place Lukan theology (which is primarily historical) above Pauline theology. I do not think this is the case. Rather, I think that charismatics place *all* of the New Testament writings on an equal footing. And is that so bad? I understand that the Book of Acts is a narrative historical account and that the Epistles are the basis for church doctrine. However, "All scripture is given by inspiration of God . . ." (2 Tim. 3:16). *All* of it is profitable for doctrine. The deeper issue is actually the authority of Scripture and certainly all evangelicals, charismatics and noncharismatics alike, would agree with the great Reformation tenet of *Sola Scriptura* (only the Scripture). We must understand that the charismatic question is one of interpretation, not of authority base.

Charismatics have often been accused of placing personal experiences and/or prophetic utterances on a higher plane than Scripture itself. I believe there is an equal danger among many traditional evangelicals who dissect the New Testament into "important" and "less important" parts. Can it be that for all the traditional evangelical's talk of fidelity to the Scriptures, it is actually the charismatic who is more faithful to the whole of God's written revelation?

Certainly one of the most disconcerting experiences in the Christian life is to see God moving outside one's own group. This seems to be an especially unnerving experience for conservative evangelicals, because they tend to be so highly ethnocentric. But God will not be boxed in! God the Spirit is moving in the church both inside and outside charismatic circles, and nothing you or I can say will stop it! In fact, when those belligerent to charismatic phenomena begin to speak against it, it grows all the more. I reiterate that the best way to insure an outbreak of tongues in any church is to

83

preach against it! It is often those who preach out the most "boldly" against the "charismatic threat" who are actually the most scared.

If we really want to be bold on this issue, then let's be bold enough to tell the whole truth. The real truth is that there are wheat and tares, the real and the fake, among charismatics. And there are wheat and tares, the real and the fake, among traditional evangelicals. Because of the human factor, there is truth mixed with error among both charismatics and noncharismatics. None of us are going to score a perfect one hundred percent on our theology when we get to heaven and hear *God's* explanation. Some charismatic services smack of emotionalism. But some traditional evangelical methods of evangelism smack of emotionalism too. It is no more wise to reject the entire charismatic movement because of its problems than it is to reject a particular evangelistic method because of the problems some people see in it.

There is a problem the church has always had with the Holy Spirit: He is unpredictable and uncontrollable by the institution. When people are filled with God's Spirit they may find themselves led in new directions. The old wineskins may burst. But this is not as much a danger as it is a hope.

While many traditional evangelicals accuse charismatics of causing friction and disunity, it is actually the narrow-mindedness of a lot of traditional evangelicals that poses the greatest threat to the unity of evangelical witness. I have found that charismatics are generally much more eager for a united evangelical front than are the traditional evangelicals.

84

Many noncharismatic evangelicals have not taken the charismatic movement seriously as a true work of God. At best they have tolerated charismatics in their churches and at worst driven them out. While charismatics are sometimes accused of being anti-local church, it is often true that they are ostracized or downright thrown out of local assemblies. Often noncharismatic evangelicals have *forced* charismatics to find their fellowship with some other group.

There has not been an exercise of mature leadership in the matter. I challenge the mature noncharismatic pastor to integrate the charismatic movement into the life of the church and stop treating those who speak in tongues like spiritual lepers. The traditional evangelical deplores the exclusivism of charismatics who say that only those who speak in tongues are truly Spirit-filled. But this traditional evangelical is often discriminatory in reverse. Such a person attempts to keep the charismatic at a safe distance away from the life of the church. As a result the local body is not blessed. Rather, it suffers.

If indeed the pastor has faithfully taught his people and grounded them in the Word of God, he need not fear. The congregation will be mature enough to gratefully accept what is genuinely a work of God and to discard all manifestations that are not truly scriptural.

Many traditional evangelicals find themselves in the role of Bunyan's Mr. Valiant For Truth. This is admirable, especially in a day when truth ("true truth" as Francis Schaeffer calls it) is being molested on all sides. However, Mr. Valiant should ask himself, "Am I really trying to uphold the purity of the Word of God or am I just trying to defend my position, or worse yet my own dead orthodoxy?" While orthodox *doctrine* must always be defended, dead orthodoxy, going through the motions, should not be defended but instead discarded. I am a traditionalist at many points, but I do not see the wisdom of beating a dead horse, especially when the Lord keeps knocking at the door of His church asking for entrance (see Rev. 3:20). If and when we truly let Him in, we must be prepared for the unexpected. He is, after all, a very creative God. The sad fact is that many noncharismatic evangelicals preach marvelous truths, but they preach them with no anointing and no power. They are like clouds without rain. The church today needs the charismatic element.

I have nothing against a defense of the faith. In fact, it is one of the most needed ministries of our generation, and I myself am involved in it. But I would especially ask my evangelical friends who want to defend the purity of Christian faith that they begin by fighting the right enemy. The enemy in the conservative denominations is not the charismatic—it is the theological liberal! Yet many conservatives are fighting the wrong enemy. They chastize the charismatic day and night, yet they turn as if blind from the obvious encroachment of liberals into their schools, departments, and commissions. When will noncharismatic evangelicals learn that the charismatic evangelical is their friend? He too is a biblical conservative. If evangelical denominations are to preserve their conservative, biblical heritage then all conservatives within the denomination must unite together. That will mean (horror of horrors and blessing of blessings) that charismatics and noncharismatics who love the Word of God and who are true to it will *have to* lock hands together. To me that sounds like a group of kids about to experience their first roller coaster ride. It's a sweet sight. They look at each other and giggle, wondering what to expect. They mutually face the challenge of the unknown. It's kind of scary and fun at the same time—together.

9

Doctrine Vs. Experience

Christian doctrine and Christian experience are inseparably intertwined. Yet it seems to be our nature to desire a dichotomy. We are always trying to back God into an either/or situation. But God will not be cornered. It is really not a question of either doctrine or experience. It is most properly a question of both doctrine and experience.

However, in theology we must try to boil things down to their least common denominator. And we must determine a base of authority. When all is said and done we must conclude that either the Bible is our final authority, or something other than the Bible is our final authority.

There are two classical approaches to theology within evangelicalism. One is often labeled a "theology of the Word." Its focus is upon the objective body of Christian truth as revealed to us in the Scriptures. Another approach to theology could be termed a "theology of experience," or as it is sometimes referred to, "relational theology." The theology of the Word has its trinitarian focus on Christ while the theology of experience has its trinitarian focus on the Holy Spirit.

Most evangelicals—including charismatics—

have held to a theology of the Word. Some evangelicals—including charismatics—are enamored with the theology of experience. Still the question must be asked: "Is there not a way to integrate the theology of the Word and the theology of experience?" I believe there is.

No one would have been more concerned that Christian truth be based on objective historical data than the apostle Paul. He clearly preached and taught that faith is founded on facts. Peter expressed the same thing when he said, "We have not followed cunningly devised fables, when we made known unto you the power and coming of our Lord Jesus Christ, but we were eyewitnesses to His majesty" (2 Pet. 1:16). The historical accountability in the witness of the apostles is evident throughout the New Testament. The early preachers invited their hearers to inspect the historical validity of the claims they made regarding Jesus' death and resurrection. Yet with all of Paul's concern for objectivity he stated that the whole purpose of his life was "That I may know Him" (Phil. 3:10). In other words, Paul desired deep experiences with God. Jesus prayed, "This is life eternal, that they might know thee the only true God and Jesus Christ, whom thou hath sent" (John 17:3). Here again our Lord declares that eternal life is not only based in data but in experience.

Actually Christ made it clear that the Scriptures alone were not sufficient to produce a knowledge of God, though they do present infallible truth about God. He rebuked the Jews for their faith only in His written revelation instead of His Person. He said,

"You search the Scriptures, because you think that in them you have eternal life; and it is these that bear witness of Me." (John 5:39, NASB).

The unfortunate facts are these. Too many charismatics have legitimate, valid experiences with God while retaining a shallow and sometimes faulty theology. Too many traditional evangelicals have tidy doctrine and truncated experience. I believe one of the great breakthroughs theologically in this century would be for someone to develop a theology that would integrate the theology of the Word with the theology of experience.

When all is said and done we can only have one final authority. That authority will be either our experience or the Bible. Our experiences should always line up perfectly with God's Word. Unfortunately, this does not always happen. In fact, this is one of the important reasons that there had to be a canon of Scripture in the first place. We need a God-given commentary as a check on ourselves. The Bible supplies that need.

This raises the all-important question: Are our experiences a commentary on our doctrine or is our doctrine a commentary on our experiences? Is the validity of our doctrine founded upon the validity of our experiences or vice versa? Our desire and duty as Christians are to know God in all of His fullness. But this purpose is to be understood in Scripture first and then in experience. I was able to experience the saving work of Christ only *after* I had been told about it. There must be a presentation of truth before truth can be experienced. And truth cannot be presented unless we know what the truth is.

It is at this point that the doctrine of experience can become very dangerous. It is closely akin to neoorthodoxy. Neoorthodoxy states that the Bible *becomes* the Word of God as it is validated by our own experience. On the other hand, evangelicals have historically contended that the Bible *is* the Word of God whether our experience validates it or not. When all is said and done we have to make a choice between the two schools of thought. Our authority will have to be either experience or doctrine. If we are to have a sound faith that will stand the pressures and tests of time, then our faith must follow this order: first doctrine, then experience. That is, we must move from the Word to experience not from experience to the Word.

The Bible is its own best commentary. It stands as the only purely objective piece of writing in all of the world regarding God and man. Since it was penned by holy men of God who were in fact moved along by the Holy Spirit as they wrote, we have an objective word as to the nature of man and a truthful word as to the nature of God. We therefore must judge all experience by this objective data that God has left for us. If we move away from the Bible as our final authority for all matters, then it is anyone's guess as to who or what should control our religious experiences. Your experience is as good as mine. My experience is as good as yours. If we don't have some outside objective authority to tell us what is true and what is false, then "every man will do what is right in his own eyes." The result is religious anarchy. In the deceitfulness of his heart man has always wanted this kind of religious system; do it however you like it. Approach God in the way you think is best. In short, do your own thing. But God does not give us this option.

This manner of thinking came to a head early in the history of the human race with the tragic story of Cain and Abel. Cain did what was right according to Cain. Cain was not concerned with the objective word of God regarding acceptable sacrifices, but rather he desired to approach God in a way that suited him. Abel was obedient to God in that he came to God on God's terms. The result was that God honored Abel's sacrifice and was displeased with Cain's. Cain rejected God's way. He rejected the doctrine of blood. As a result he ended up shedding blood.

It's the same story today. A depraved, perverse world, with a thirst and thrill for the bloody, rejects our Bible faith as being primitive. They reject the message of the Cross. And because they reject the message of the shed blood they increasingly shed blood.

Our natural inclination is to want to come to God our own way. It seems easy and convenient to agree with those who say, "It doesn't matter what you believe as long as you are sincere." Obviously the problem is that one can be sincerely wrong. A man may take a dosage of medicine, sincerely thinking it will help him get better. However, if he takes the wrong medicine tragic consequences may result.

I am reminded of the story of the little boy in Sunday school who was asked by his teacher, "Jimmy, what is false doctrine?" "False doctorin'," said Jimmy, "is giving the wrong medicine to sick people."

He was a lot closer to the truth than he knew! It is

not enough to be sincere. We must have the truth. And to have truth we must have objective data. Fortunately we do have it—in the Bible.

It would be my hope that by the time this book is published the Holy Spirit will have sent a healing breeze across the church. Without a doubt it is past time for the church to experience a charismatic truce. We need to move beyond the charismatic issue. There is a much greater and much more important issue facing evangelicalism.

In my opinion, the issue with the most far-reaching implications for evangelicalism is the issue of biblical inerrancy. In importance, the charismatic question runs far behind the inerrancy issue. This is because the charismatic issue is a question of interpretation, while the question of biblical infallibility cuts to the very heart of authority itself.

I, for one, believe it is possible to try all experiences by the objective, written Word of God while still experiencing the power and anointing of the Holy Spirit. Evangelicals must relearn that true fulfillment in life comes not from knowledge about God but from knowledge of God. We are never fulfilled until we experience God. Augustine said, "Our hearts are restless until they find their rest in Thee." Pascal said, "There is a God-shaped vacuum in every human heart." But these experiences with God must line up with Scripture. We cannot be like the addict who claims to have found God through drugs or like the mystic who claims to know God through transcendental meditation.

We may say we are much too biblical in our approach to God to fall prey to those traps. Perhaps.

But there is a much more deceptive pitfall in which many Christians are ensnared. It is entirely possible to begin to worship doctrines and creeds that are true instead of worshiping the true and living God.

Martha experienced this problem when Jesus came to the tomb of her brother Lazarus. Jesus asked her if she believed in the resurrection. She answered the Lord in a perfectly orthodox and correct way. She said, "Yes, Lord. I know that my brother will rise in the last day." Jesus reminded Martha that a belief in the resurrection was not based on the writings of the prophets primarily, but rather on the fact of His own resurrection and that He would become the firstfruits of all those who sleep. He reminded Martha, "*I* am the resurrection and the life" (John 11:25, emphasis mine). Our hope is not in the written word but in the living Word. We must translate the Scripture into living, vital experience. We must *experience* God. Our lives are changed as we know Him through communion with Him. But all such experience, all sensations and "words from the Lord," must be checked by the objective teaching of the Scriptures.

Some time ago a woman came to me for counsel concerning her marital problems. She was a Christian, but her husband was not. I asked her if she had been warned before her marriage that as a Christian she should not marry an unbeliever and if she had known the Bible teaching which says believers are not to enter into a marital union with unbelievers (see 2 Cor. 6:14). Her answer to me was reflective of the problem we are facing. She said, "Oh, yes. I know what the Bible teaches. But a prophet of God prophesied over me and told me that I should go

95

ahead and marry this man. So I obeyed the prophecy." This sincere woman had been fooled and tricked by a false prophet. She was led to believe that a supposed spoken word from God in the twentieth century could nullify the written Word of God of the first century. This will never be the case.

Never think for a minute that God is about to change His mind regarding any written injunction from the Bible. The Bible tells us this about God's character: "For I am the Lord, I change not . . ." (Mal. 3:6). If He gave us instructions two thousand years ago, the principles upon which the instructions were given have not changed nor will they. There are continually changing cultural norms and derivatives; however, there also is valid, objective, final truth for all generations. Such is biblical truth for ". . . his [God's] truth endureth to all generations" (Ps. 100:5). There is such a thing as final truth.

If you have placed experience as a higher criterion for faith than the objective data of the Bible, you are in trouble. If you have allowed yourself to covet experiences while remaining scripturally ignorant, you are in double trouble. You have opened the door to contact with every sect, cult, and demonic illusion known to man. My advice to you is to get back to the Bible. And quick.

The Taylor-Johnson Temperament Analysis Test is given to determine certain personality tendencies. According to the test the most important trait for mental and emotional health is a high degree of objectivity. The more objective a person is the healthier he will be emotionally. The same is true in our theology. The more objective we are, the healthier our theology will be.

All experience is subjective because of the human element. And subjectivity is not entirely bad. It only becomes bad when it does not have the check of objective data to determine its validity. Therefore, a healthy Christian life-style is one of daily, fresh experiences with the Lord; communion with God that is new every morning—but all of it stacking up in agreement with the written, objective Word of God.

A theology of the Word? A theology of experience? I propose a theology of the Word that leads to experience. Without experience we may know about God, but we will never know Him personally. Without sound doctrine we will never know whether we really know God. It is the Spirit that draws us to Christ, and it is that same Holy Spirit who keeps drawing us to Christ, after conversion as well as before. The Holy Spirit ever points us to Jesus, both before and after we are saved. When we were converted we heard the historically verifiable message of the death, burial, and resurrection of Jesus. "So then faith cometh by hearing, and hearing by the Word of God" (Rom. 10:17). We were brought to saving faith by both the Spirit and the Word. Jesus declared that Christians are born of the Spirit (see John 3:6). Peter declared that Christians are born of the Word. (1 Pet. 1:23). But while it is the Spirit who brings us together, it is like precious faith that keeps us together.

10

Mr. Jones, Meet the Holy Spirit

To many people I am an enigma. Charismatics, more often than not, refer to me as noncharismatic while many traditional evangelicals label me as charismatic. Many folks have cornered me and asked me, "Are you a charismatic?" Well of course I'm a charismatic in the biblical sense of the word. All Christians are. I have gifts bestowed on me by the Holy Spirit as do all of God's children. In that sense I am a charismatic—as are all other Christians. But, no, I am not always in agreement with the majority views of the charismatic movement.

Perhaps the question as to whether or not I'm a charismatic could best be answered in a little more detail. Most of my differences with the charismatic movement are more philosophical than theological, though I do have some doctrinal differences with the "typical" charismatic, if there is such a creature. Yes, I'm a charismatic if that is one who believes that all of the gifts of the Spirit are still in operation today just as they were in the early church. No, I'm not a charismatic if that is one who believes it is imperative for a person to speak in tongues to be filled with the Spirit. Yes, I'm a charismatic if that is one who believes that we should never limit the power of God in any way, shape, or fashion. No, I'm not a charismatic if that is one who seeks for thrills and experiences at the expense of a daily, noneventful walk toward Christian maturity. Yes, I'm a charismatic if that is one who believes that the gifts of the Spirit are sorely needed to revitalize the church today. No, I'm not a charismatic if that is one who believes that the gifts of the Spirit are more important than the fruit of the Spirit.

But, after all, God is not so concerned about our labels. There isn't a Baptist Holy Spirit and a Pentecostal Holy Spirit, a Christian Businessmen's Committee Holy Spirit and Full Gospel Business Men's Holy Spirit, a Campus Crusade Holy Spirit and a Teen Challenge Holy Spirit. There's only *one* Holy Spirit! When we get to heaven I am sure that the Father will not want to know if we were "charismatic." He *will* want to know if we lived a life controlled by the Holy Spirit.

Here again I find myself with one foot in each camp. Or maybe I should say with one foot outside each camp. I find some charismatic gatherings rather repugnant. The carnival atmosphere that prevails as people sit around and watch others "get the baptism" turns me off. I personally do not believe that the filling of the Holy Spirit is a mail order, mass production operation. Consequently I am skeptical of the walk-down-the-line, lay-your-hands-on-the-candidate approach to receiving God's fullness. It seems that too often people are seeking the thrill of the fill rather than the fullness of God. Too often I have seen folks more expectant of the touch of man than the touch of God.

From the experiences of many great Christian

leaders of the past and present I must conclude that the experience of being filled with the Holy Spirit is, more often than not, a very private, sacred occurrence. Far from wanting to tell the world all the details of their experience, Finney, Moody, Spurgeon, and others were most reticent about publicly describing the details of their intimate baptism in the Spirit. As Moody stated, "Oh, what a day! I cannot describe it, I seldom refer to it; it is almost too sacred an experience to name."[1]

While detesting the frivolity with which many in charismatic circles approach this sacred experience, I also am unhappy with the common evangelical approach to receiving the filling of the Spirit. I call it the ABC method. It seems that many have made it such a cut and dried occurrence that they have stripped this precious experience of its uniqueness, color, and power. Many evangelical Bible teachers, while instructing those who wish to be filled with the Spirit, say things like, "Don't expect an emotional experience." Why shouldn't they? They are about to be filled with the Spirit of the living God! I agree that one can be filled with the Holy Spirit without an accompanying experience of high emotion, but I also know that an emotional response to the invasion of the fullness of God into our lives would certainly be nothing out of the ordinary.

I have also heard evangelicals say, "Don't expect any manifestation. Don't expect, for instance, to speak in tongues." Why shouldn't they? Certainly not all of those in the Book of Acts who were filled with the Spirit spoke in tongues—but some of them did. Wouldn't it be safer to say, "Do whatever the Spirit bids you to do. Some will speak in tongues;

others won't. Some may have another manifestation of the Spirit; others may experience no manifestation at all. Let the Holy Spirit deal with you as an individual." Believers with a traditional orientation should be prepared to speak in tongues if that is how the Spirit directs them. Believers with a charismatic orientation should be prepared *not* to speak in tongues if that is how the Spirit directs them.

So here again I sometimes feel like a man without a country. I am uneasy with both the charismatic carnival method and the evangelical ABC method. What I prefer is the biblical method. I am convinced that the biblical method regarding the baptism or filling of the Holy Spirit does not place the emphasis on the receiving but on the preparation to receive.

It must be remembered that the Christian is not being instructed to "receive the Holy Spirit." He already has the Holy Spirit. Paul said in Romans 8:9 that ". . . if any man have not the Spirit of Christ, he is none of his." The Bible clearly teaches that we are "sealed with the holy Spirit" until "the day of redemption" (Eph. 1:13, 4:30). Clearly all Christians have the Holy Spirit residing in them.

This does not mean, however, that all Christians are filled with the Holy Spirit. If this were true there would have been no need for Paul to command believers to be filled with the Holy Spirit (see Eph. 5:18). In all reverence we must conclude that if indeed all Christians are filled with the Holy Spirit the Spirit is not making a very big impact upon a lost world. But the salient truth is that most Christians are not filled with the Holy Spirit. It is as one writer stated: "I used to believe that a few men had a monopoly on the Holy Spirit. I have since learned that the Holy Spirit has a monopoly on a few men."

If a greater percentage of Christians were experiencing the fullness of God's Spirit, a much greater impact would be made on our world for Christ. Jesus said, "But ye shall receive power after that the Holy Ghost is come upon you: and ye shall be witnesses unto me" (Acts 1:8). It is glaring from this passage that an evidence of being filled with the Spirit is powerful witness for Christ. To be filled with the Holy Spirit is simply to abide in Christ and the result is that we will bear much fruit.

We must always remember that to be filled with the Holy Spirit is not so much a one-time experience as it is a way of life. We must keep in mind that we are not told only to be filled with the Spirit but also to walk in the Spirit; that is, to allow the Holy Spirit to control us moment by moment.

There are three terms that I believe are synonymous. They are the "lordship of Christ," "abiding in Christ," and "filled with the Spirit." If one is filled with the Spirit, Jesus is his Lord. If one is abiding in Christ, Christ is Lord of every area of his life. If one is abiding in Christ, he is filled with the Holy Spirit. To abide in Christ is to experience His lordship. To experience Christ's lordship is to be filled with the Spirit. To experience Christ's lordship is to abide in Christ. To be filled with the Holy Spirit is to experience Christ's lordship. To be filled with the Holy Spirit is to abide in Christ.

There's really nothing mystical nor magical about the baptism or filling of the Holy Spirit. Really it all boils down to one thing: surrender. Without a surrender of our will to the will of God we

103

will never be filled with the Holy Spirit. We may receive gifts of the Spirit, just as many had at Corinth, and remain carnal. We may speak in tongues and think that we have "the baptism." But in fact, if our will has not been surrendered we don't have any such thing. We need to learn that the Bible is talking about two different subjects when it refers to the filling of the Spirit and the gifts of the Spirit. They may overlap. They often do. But they are two distinct entities. Surrender is the name of the game, and for most of us surrender is more involved than we may think.

It is true that to surrender and consecrate our lives to Christ only takes a second. It can be done in a moment of time. However, the mental and spiritual struggles leading up to that surrender of every aspect of one's life to Christ's lordship may take days, weeks, or even months. That is why I am cautious of the high-spirited new Christian—who knows nothing of taking up the cross, nothing of being crucified with Christ, nothing of the fellowship of His suffering, and nothing of being made conformable to His death—being shoved through a line of "seekers" and thrust into an experience that he really knows nothing about. Anything that is worth anything has a price tag on it. To know God in His fullness costs. There's a price to be paid. And it's not cheap.

Many feel that the baptism in the Holy Spirit (or "filling" if you prefer) will bring joy and power into their lives. This is wonderfully true. But joy and power is not all that being filled with the Spirit will bring into your life! If one is filled with God's Spirit he will be thrust into situations that the natural man is completely incapable of handling. He will do battle with the forces of darkness. He will come against the spirit of the age and the workers of iniquity. And sometimes he will even fight against demonic forces and evil of every kind.

This led one great Christian to wisely remark that most Christians who seek to be filled with the Spirit, if they really knew what they were asking, would change their prayer to this: "Oh God do anything in my life that you want except to fill me with the Spirit! Take me and do anything you want. Just don't fill me with the Spirit."[2]

It is true that your ministry will be increased when you are filled with the Holy Spirit. It is also true that your opposition will be increased. There will be new opportunities and new challenges. There will be fresh adventure and fresh pain. But after your life on this earth is over you will be able to say, "It was worth it, for I have walked with the Lord."

The happy truth is that at salvation you get all of the Holy Spirit that you're ever going to get. The sad truth is that so often at salvation people give the Holy Spirit all of themselves that He is ever going to get! What should occur is that every day, yes, every moment, we give all that we know about ourselves to all that we know about God, and as a result experience a continual flow of God's power.

Again I remind you that the key is surrender. God never fills anyone with His Spirit who has unconfessed sin in his life. God never fills anyone with His Spirit who harbors resentment. God will not share His glory with anyone else. The Spirit will not possess a man who is possessed with pride. To be filled with the Holy Spirit is to experience what John the Baptist said: "He must increase, but I must decrease" (John 3:30). The key is total surrender. As Martin Luther once said, "He wants to teach you not how the Spirit comes to you but how you come to the Spirit."

You may be asking, "What is the evidence of being filled with the Holy Spirit?" The answer is that the evidence will vary from person to person. In the Book of Acts each reference to speaking in tongues is related to the filling of the Holy Spirit. But there are thirteen references in Acts either to receiving or being filled with the Holy Spirit. Only three of these occurrences refer to speaking in tongues. Another evidence of being filled with the Holy Spirit is that you will sing and make melody in your heart to the Lord. You will give thanks and you will submit to other believers. Paul describes exactly what will happen as a consequence of the Spirit's fullness in Ephesians 5:18-21. Notice that the consequences he mentions are all moral qualities:

> And be not drunk with wine, wherein is excess; but be filled with the Spirit; Speaking to yourselves in psalms and hymns and spiritual songs, singing and making melody in your heart to the Lord; Giving thanks always for all things unto God and the Father in the name of our Lord Jesus Christ; Submitting yourselves one to another in the fear of God.

Final, definite evidence of being filled with the Holy Spirit is an incessant desire to tell people, not about your baptism in the Spirit, but about Jesus.

When one is filled with the Holy Spirit it is inconceivable that he would not tell people about Christ.

It may seem like a simple answer, but the fact is, you will know when you are filled with the Holy Spirit. You won't need anyone to verify it for you or to decide for you whether or not you have been filled. You will just know, and that knowledge comes from faith in God's Word.

———————

[1]John R. Rice, *The Power of Pentecost* (Murfreesboro, Tenn.: Sword of the Lord Publishers, 1949) p. 393.
[2]Attributed to D. L. Moody.

11

Healing Love

Three of the great forces in Christendom today are the evangelicals, the charismatics and the liberals. I call myself, at least partially, in two of those categories (evangelical and charismatic). As I have stated earlier, the traditional evangelicals stress the teaching and preaching of the Word. The liberals stress social action. The charismatics stress miracles and signs. Each group believes that his activity is the most important element within the church. Each believes that his activity is most important in making the world Christian. But I call to your attention again the threefold evangelistic strategy of the apostle Paul. It included all three elements. In other words, Paul felt that all three—the Word, deeds, and signs—were important in reaching the world with the message of Christ.

As the close of this book approaches I can almost envisage some of the responses. Some charismatics will say, "Well he just doesn't know. He's never spoken in tongues." The fact is, I have spoken in tongues and I do speak in tongues. In my case it was the gift I experienced when I surrendered my will to the Lord and was personally filled with the Spirit, and it was not just a one-time occurrence. In fact, I

109

probably exercise the gift more frequently than do many charismatics. Yet God has directed me (and I'm confident this is in keeping with Paul's teaching to the Corinthians) to restrain all of my experiences of praying in tongues to private devotional times. I gratefully stand as proof that one can have the gift of tongues and not cause division. I have preached often in Baptist churches, Bible churches, and churches of other noncharismatic denominations. Always my message has been Christ and Him crucified, not tongues and them magnified. Always my intention has been to be a blessing, not a blunder, to the local church I was ministering to.

I would hasten to say that it was *my* experience that when I was filled with the Spirit it was accompanied by speaking in tongues. It would be unscriptural for me to impose this experience on others as a norm for receiving the baptism or filling of the Holy Spirit.

Some traditional evangelicals will say, "He's been too lenient with the charismatics. He doesn't understand the division and strife caused through this movement." The fact is, I have been a pastor, and though not frequently, I have had to deal with the misuse of gifts of the Spirit. As a pastor I experienced the sticky situations that confront so many today. In addition, for several years I pastored a transdenominational church made up of both charismatics and noncharismatics.

So, I have shared with you out of my knowledge of and experience with the issues presented in this book. My plea is for a charismatic truce, and to that end I offer the following suggestions to both groups with the prayer that they will produce healing love.

1. *Acknowledge that all the gifts of the spirit are in operation today.* Though sometimes they are misused and blown out of proportion, the truth remains that God is pouring out His Spirit in these last days upon all flesh.

2. *Realize that God fills people with His Spirit in a variety of ways.* The evidence of being filled with the Holy Spirit is not so much speaking in another tongue as it is controlling the tongue you have! You may speak in tongues, or you may receive another gift of the Spirit. You may just have the calm assurance of God's power and renewal in your life. God evidently enjoys being diverse.

3. *Grieve not the Spirit.* The Holy Spirit is grieved by immoral, unethical, or unloving conduct in the life of Christians. While the Christians at Corinth were blessed with all spiritual gifts the Holy Spirit Himself was deeply grieved because of the factuous spirit and rampant immorality among those who claimed high spiritual endowments.

4. *Quench not the Spirit.* It is a dangerous thing to suppress the movement of the Spirit of God. There is a fresh breath of the Holy Spirit sweeping across America and the world. I would consider my ministry a failure if I didn't move with the Spirit of God. It can be unsettling, but it is always exciting to allow the Holy Spirit free reign in our personal lives and in the lives of our churches.

5. *Strive for biblical unity.* The prayer of our Lord Jesus for us was "that they may be one." I am con-

vinced He was not speaking of an organizational unity but rather of a spiritual unity. It is possible to be organizationally united and spiritually divided. Conversely it is also possible to be spiritually united while maintaining denominational and independent distinctives. It is my personal feeling that this latter kind of unity is much more pleasing to God. It is not only possible to love Christians of all backgrounds, persuasions, and colors—it is a biblical mandate.

6. *Weigh your words carefully.* The Bible teaches that we will give an account for every idle word. I urge charismatics to use the term "Spirit-filled" in a more discerning way. Let it refer to all those whose lives express the fruit of the Spirit and all those who are living under the lordship of Christ, not just to those who have had an experience similar to theirs. Refer to all evangelical churches as full gospel churches, for indeed they are. Every church that preaches salvation through the blood, based upon the death, burial, and resurrection of the Lord, according to 1 Corinthians 15:3,4 is a full gospel church.

I urge noncharismatics to drop from their vocabulary the term "tongues movement." This is not a proper description of what is actually taking place in the lives of thousands of believers who do in fact speak in tongues. It is much broader than just tongues.

Finally, I would encourage charismatics to refer to the "infilling of the Holy Spirit" instead of the "baptism in the Holy Spirit" when in dialogue with other evangelicals. Although this may be purely a matter of semantics, it will help the process of communication, which is so important.

7. *Share your experiences selectively.* This goes for both charismatics and traditional evangelicals. Your private experiences should remain that way. If your walk with the Lord is deep enough, some things will be too beautiful and too sacred for public display. Remember, if you are really filled with the Holy Spirit you won't have to tell anybody. We will all know.

8. *Make evangelism your priority.* Let's not forget that the Great Commission of our Lord is to go and make disciples out of every nation, baptizing them and teaching them to observe all things that He has commanded us. All evangelicals—charismatics and noncharismatics alike—can and must lock arms together in a great final thrust to preach the gospel to every creature. This will take all of our energies. It will take the empowering of the Holy Spirit in all of us to get the job done. If we are talking more about our denomination or our experience than we are about redemption in Christ, our priorities are dead wrong.

9. *Submit to your pastor.* Remember that God has placed your pastor over you to encourage, exhort, and protect you. More often than not your pastor will possess spiritual sensitivity beyond the average layman. Don't work against him, work with him. He loves you, he intercedes for you and your family. Work with him. You're on the same team.

113

10. *Ask God for a teachable spirit.* Again this goes for both charismatics and noncharismatics. Both groups have an integral and exciting contribution to make to church-body life. We need the instruction and insight of all believers.

11. *Share your doctrinal insights in love, not in a reactionary spirit.* Unfortunately both groups have reacted *against* the statements of the other. If a brother is in doctrinal error, ". . . ye which are spiritual *restore* such an one . . ." (Gal. 6:1, emphasis mine). Restore, don't react.

12. *Realize that God is bigger than you and your doctrinal system.* God is at work all over the place. He is at work in your church and in the church down the street. He loves all of His children (all of the world for that matter) and He is working in all believers to conform us to His image.

13. *Learn from all evangelical Bible teachers and preachers.* This is not to say that we should not discern false doctrine. We should not swallow everything that everybody says hook, line, and sinker But do not discredit any man's entire ministry simply because you may disagree with one thing he says. If he is straight on the salvation message, give him some slack. I have profited greatly from the ministries of Oral Roberts and Billy Graham, David Wilkerson and W. A. Criswell, Pat Robertson and Bill Bright, C. M. Ward and Ian Thomas; not to mention many others. Though I may not agree with all the statements I've heard these men make, I am still grateful for the unique contribution that each of them has made to my Christian life.

14. *Fight the right enemy.* The traditional evangelical is not your enemy, he is your brother. The charismatic is not your enemy, he is your brother. In a real sense, even the liberal is not your enemy. Rather, the theological liberal is a victim of the enemy. Your real enemy is Satan, as Peter warned: ". . . your adversary the devil, as a roaring lion, walketh about, seeking whom he may devour" (1 Pet. 5:8). All Christians need to band together and fight the right enemy.

15. *Love one another.* The mark of the Christian is love. When all is said and done and the charismatic issue settles in the dust of time, the final observation will not be whether or not we were charismatic but to what degree we loved one another.

* * *

Our God we worship You: Father, Son, and Holy Spirit. We are grateful that You have called us into Your family. We ask that You would break our pride and show us Your mighty works. Visit us with a fresh invasion of Your Spirit and give us grace to acknowledge it and receive it with thanksgiving. Make us always true to Your Word and lead us toward the true unity that You desire for us. Beyond all and above all let us love one another, for love is from You. May we know the love of Christ, which passes knowledge. Lead us, Father, into a new day of appreciation and cooperation for the higher goals of world evangelization that surpass all sectarianism and carnal strife. Teach us what it really means to be filled with Your Spirit in the name of our Lord Jesus Christ, He who is our peace. Amen.